A MEMOIR INSPIRED BY
THE LIFE OF **GAYLYNN KAPRI**

GET UP

*A Story of One
Woman's Journey
and The God Who
Wouldn't Let Go*

LaVonne M. Chastain

Get Up!

One Woman's Journey and the God Who Wouldn't Let Go

A Memoir Inspired by the Life of Gaylynn Kapri

by LaVonne M. Chastain

For permission requests, contact the publisher at:

Valley Grace Publishing

valleygracepub@gmail.com

This is a work of nonfiction. The stories and reflections are based on the real experiences of the author and contributor. Names and identifying details may have been changed to protect privacy.

Cover and Interior design by Jennifer Stimson

Photo Credits: All family photographs are from the personal collection of the author and used with permission.

Stock images are sourced from licensed providers or free stock sites such as Unsplash and Pixabay

Printed in the United States of America

Published by Valley Grace Publishing

Paperback ISBN 979-8-9932742-0-1

Hardcover ISBN 979-8-9932742-1-8

Ebook ISBN 979-8-9932742-2-5

Author's Note

This is a true story, written with deep respect for both the beauty and the brokenness of a life lived with courage. While many of the events in this memoir are drawn from real experiences, I have intentionally chosen not to include the names of some individuals.

This decision was made not to minimize anyone's impact or importance, but to honor privacy, especially in cases involving trauma, abuse, or painful family history.

A gentle note for readers: These pages include references to abuse, trauma, addiction, profound loss, and serious illness. I have tried to handle each with honesty and tenderness. If you need to pause, please do. May you also find here evidence of courage, community, and our God who meets us in the broken places.

What matters most here is not who, but how: how one woman endured, how faith carried her, and how light was found even in the darkest corners.

Where needed, relationships are described through roles—mother, sister, daughter, husband, friend—rather than by name. These choices are intentional and made with both reverence and restraint.

This is Gaylynn's story. Told in truth, told with love, and told with the hope that it may offer healing to others.

CONTENTS

PROLOGUE

"But he took her by the hand and said,
'My child, get up!'" — Luke 8:54

This story has been stirring in our hearts for nearly a decade. For as long as I can remember, Gaylynn and I talked about writing a book together someday—our book. The first time she said, "We should write a book," we were driving in my car, laughing so hard at childhood memories that tears streamed down our faces. She loved to tease me about my silly quirks, while I reminded her of her eagerness to practice kissing a boy using the mirror in my bedroom. We especially delighted in recalling visits to our grandparents' house—our grandmother's contagious laugh, and the pride she took in growing her rose bushes. That day, between bursts of laughter, Gaylynn leaned in, eyes sparkling, and said it again, not as a joke this time. "This will make a great chapter in our book!" For her, the vision was instant. For me, it took root quietly, settling somewhere in the back of my mind until God brought it forward in His time.

When she said we should write a book, I always knew what she really meant was I should write it. She had the story—the life, the scars, the triumphs—but she needed someone to give it voice. Anyone who knows Gaylynn knows she does not have the patience for details or the discipline required to put pen to paper. That's just not her gift. But she has a way of drawing people into her dreams, convincing them—with that mix of charm, persistence, and unshakable energy—to help her make them real.

Gaylynn has always wanted to share her journey—not for attention, but with the hope that it might offer someone else the courage to keep going, that it might breathe life into a weary soul who believes their story is already over. If you've ever been there, standing in a season where hope felt far away, you'll understand why she couldn't keep this to herself. Her intent has never been to be seen as a victim, as some might suggest; far from it. Above all else, she is a fighter. And that will become abundantly clear as you turn the pages of this book. But Gaylynn is so much more than just someone who survived. The layers of her life—both the heartache and the healing—have shaped her into someone extraordinary. She is loving, compassionate, kind-hearted, funny, thoughtful, fiercely determined, strong-willed, and undeniably stubborn.

My prayer throughout this process has been that whatever I put on paper would represent her well, bless you the reader, and allow you to feel the heartbeat of this story—not just as words, but as a testimony of two women bound by blood and held even more tightly by the grace and love of our heavenly Father.

As you read through the intricacies of a delicate, beautiful, and many times painful life, I pray you'll find moments of laughter, glimmers of joy, and yes, more than a few tears. Please remember, dear reader, that the stories in these pages are told from memory, spanning from childhood to adulthood, and may not reflect the intentions or perspectives of others involved at the time. Writing this often made me think of the Gospels—one truth, told through different lenses. What you're about to read is our perspective. And like all perspectives, it shapes not only what we remember, but who we become. That's exactly what happened to both of us.

I hope one day you have the chance to meet Gaylynn in person, to witness how she lights up a room by simply walking into it, or how she instantly makes you feel like she's known you your whole life. Because once you've encountered Gaylynn Kapri, you don't easily forget her; just ask the thousands who already have. She's a whirlwind of energy, a firestorm of passion, and truly a force of nature—the kind of woman who moves through life with unrelenting devotion to others, unstoppable resilience, and a spark that refuses to be extinguished.

Please do not misunderstand me as I write this; I am by no means saying she is perfect, nor am I trying to put her up on a pedestal. Rather, I am sharing the insights and memories that have shaped her very existence and may explain her constant search for love and acceptance. She has faults just like the rest of us. She can be frustrating and difficult to understand at times. But at her core, she is kind, genuine, and deeply loving. Those who cross paths with Gaylynn are never the same. And if you already know her, I hope this story helps you to appreciate her, perhaps forgive her, and prayerfully walk away with a deeper understanding of who she really is, the impossible decisions she has had to make, and why she now lives her life as a champion for others.

Make no mistake: Gaylynn and I have had our moments of frustration, anger, and even seasons of mistrust. But in the midst of those times, through prayer, God spoke to my heart and gave me a choice: *Love her, or leave her.* I chose to love her, just as she is. Not everyone who faced that same crossroad has chosen to stay. That saddens me, because those who have fallen away have missed the chance to know a truly unique soul. But as most of us understand, life moves in seasons, and sometimes people are only meant to be in our lives for a time. Gaylynn willingly carries a piece of each person she has ever loved, even those who have chosen to walk away. Her heart, one of the biggest I've ever known, holds space for everyone who has entered her world, no matter how brief the encounter.

Through it all, one thing remains certain: Gaylynn rises. Even when life knocked her breathless, she found a way to move forward—sometimes crawling, sometimes running, but always reaching for what God held for her. This unshakable resolve is what brought her to where she is today. By sharing her story, she hasn't simply given us a window into her life; she has opened the door wide open for us to truly appreciate it. As you will read in her own words, she will never forget hearing God's voice telling her, *GET UP! It's not your time.*

Those words became the anchor for everything that followed . . . and it is the message at the heart of this story.

LaVonne

BEFORE THE FALL

"But Jesus came and touched them. 'Get up,' he said. 'Don't be afraid.'" — *Matthew 17:7*

The Day of Surgery — Local Hospital

The waiting room was colder than it had any right to be. Not the first-breath blast of air conditioning, but the kind of cold that seeps into you slowly—like winter pressing through an old farmhouse door. I held a cup of tea that had long gone lukewarm, watching the second hand on the wall clock jerk forward—tick, pause, tick—as if time itself were limping.

Beyond the double doors, under lights bright enough to erase every shadow, surgeons worked to cut away the tumor that had invaded Gaylynn's colon. She'd been told twice now—once far from home, then again after she returned—that this would be no ordinary surgery. If the cancer had spread, there might be nothing more they could do.

I hadn't been there for the moment she first heard the word *cancer*. I only knew the sound of her voice when she called afterward, the way it trembled as she tried to make it small. *They found something*, she had said. It wasn't small. Cancer never is.

Her mother sat beside me, chattering endlessly, her hands moving in a nervous way as she talked. Her half sister came and went, pulled away by errands and children. I stayed anchored to the chair, fingers clasped so tightly in prayer my knuckles blanched, as if I could hold the pieces of her life together by sheer will. Prayer, in those long moments, was the only steady thing I had to hold on to.

Every time the OR doors swung open, my pulse jumped. Nurses. Orderlies. A custodian with a mop. The clock kept ticking.

Then the doors opened again. This time, a surgeon in scrubs stepped out, his eyes scanning the room until they found mine. He came straight toward me, the space between us narrowing to the rhythm of his footsteps, the rustle of fabric, the rubber soles against linoleum.

He stopped.

And didn't speak.

CHAPTER 1

COUSINS, COUNTRY ROADS, AND ROOT CELLARS

"Some bonds are forged not by blood alone, but by the laughter and trials we share."

The day of Gaylynn's surgery, as I sat in the waiting room watching the clock drag forward, my mind kept circling back—not only to the fear of what lay ahead, but to the girl I had always known her to be. Strong. Spirited. Unafraid to stare down what the rest of us avoided. To understand how she came to be on that operating table, you'd have to go back decades—to our shared childhood that was both a playground and a prison. A story that began long before hospital corridors and unspoken prayers. To understand Gaylynn's courage, you first have to know where she came from.

—⁓—

The roads of our childhood wound through more than fields, fences, and farmhouses; they wound through the marrow of who we were becoming. We were connected not only by blood but by the shared experience of growing up side by side. Our mothers were sisters—mine the oldest, hers the youngest. Despite the sixteen-year age gap, their bond was strong and affectionate, and that closeness naturally extended to us. Because of it, Gaylynn and I spent much of our childhood together, weaving memories that would anchor us for a lifetime.

I can't remember a time when she wasn't part of my life. She was more than family; she was my first best friend. Before life tested her in unimaginable ways, before grief and cancer carved their names into her story, there were simpler days. We ran barefoot through fields, shared secrets in the dark, and believed the world was as endless as the summer sky.

We came of age in the 1960s and '70s—a time that now feels both distant and dreamy. Childhood then seemed filled with joy, wonder, and simplicity . . . at least from where I stood. We were both raised in middle-class working families, but our homes were vastly different. I was the youngest in my family, four years older than Gaylynn, while she was the oldest in hers. We often found ourselves in the care of our grandparents, surrounded by cousins, where the backdrop of our youth was a blend of dirt roads, porch swings, and home-cooked meals.

Before her mother remarried, Gaylynn's family had been just Gaylynn, her younger sister, and their mom. Their birth father walked away from the family when Gaylynn's younger sister was only two and facing a serious health crisis. They lived in a small apartment that their mother could afford. With him gone, the three of them drew especially close. If you asked Gaylynn's mother today, she would tell you that those were her happiest years—when it was just the three of them together, making do with just enough to get by, before heartbreak and abuse became a way of life. For Gaylynn and her sister—only eighteen months apart—it was a season of forging a bond so deep it would help carry them through the hardships that lay ahead. They were two peas in a pod, sharing everything in a way only sisters can.

Neither of the girls had a relationship with their birth father, so when a stepfather arrived, everything shifted. Suddenly, they were expected to call this new man "Dad," a title that carried no easy place in their hearts.

From her earliest years, Gaylynn remembered the constant fighting between her parents—most often about money. "As a child, my life was wild and chaotic," she later told me. "I never knew when my stepdad would come home and tell us we were moving." His threats to sell everything and uproot the family weren't rare outbursts; they became the rhythm of her childhood.

After leaving their apartment, her family moved to the countryside, settling on a small farm. Eventually, they relocated to a forty-acre property with a farmhouse, trying to build something more stable. But even then, the threat of moving always hung in the air, and uncertainty followed them.

Visiting Gaylynn's house always felt like an adventure. Much of their life unfolded in the country, while mine was centered in the city. I remember the drives out there—the winding roads that seemed to hold secrets in their bends, gravel dust lingering in the air, cicadas droning as trees arched overhead like a tunnel. Outside felt like liberation; inside, life was not always so gentle.

Her stepfather's severe drinking problem, coupled with his and her mother's inability to manage money, consistently undermined the family's security. Gaylynn recalls being part of Future Farmers of America, raising animals and proudly selling them for a profit. One summer she saved enough to open her own bank account—her "savings passbook" carefully stamped with deposits. She had plans for that money, already picturing new school clothes and supplies. But when she and her mother went to make a withdrawal, the teller shook her head: The account was empty. Her mother nervously explained they'd needed a new washer and dryer, and the money was gone. It was never replaced. Gaylynn unfortunately learned at a very young age that even when you worked hard, nothing you earned was guaranteed to stay yours.

The country has a way of disguising turmoil. To outsiders, the setting was idyllic: barefoot children chasing fireflies, neighbors waving from tractors, sunsets glowing behind tree lines. But behind the thin walls of that farmhouse, unrest was constant. Violence, favoritism, and unpredictability seeped into every corner.

One of Gaylynn's most painful memories was being dragged out of bed in the middle of the night—alongside her younger sister—to search local bars for her drunken stepfather. They would haul him home, his breath thick with alcohol, stale smoke clinging to their hair, his body slumped heavy against them. A few hours later, Gaylynn would rise for school, get her sister ready, brush the smell of smoke from their clothes, and step into the day as if nothing had happened.

In that household, school was never a priority. Hard work and sheer endurance always came first. Childhood, for Gaylynn, was not a time of discovery but of survival. And yet, even in those darkest places, she held on to a quiet belief that somehow things would get better.

At the heart of both our childhoods was our grandparents' place in the country. It was no storybook farmhouse: just a cramped two-bedroom home with peeling paint, a screen door that never shut quietly, and a swamp cooler that barely worked, pushing warm, stale air around while the hundred-degree summer heat pressed in from every wall. But it was where all the cousins gathered, where laughter and love mixed with an unspoken pecking order.

Our papa would come home from the fields with dirt in his hands and produce stacked like trophies in his arms. We'd sit on the porch steps with sun-warmed tomatoes, juice dripping down our wrists. The smell of earth and fruit mingled with the dry dust that clung to everything. Those moments felt timeless: the creak of the rocker, the slant of light, the hope that maybe time could hold still.

But even there, favoritism carved its marks. Grandma openly favored me and Gaylynn's younger sister. At the time, I basked in the attention, never thinking about the shadow it cast. Only years later did I realize how it shaped Gaylynn, teaching her to work twice as hard for half as much tenderness, always one step outside the circle.

Nothing captured the favoritism more than who was sent in to grab something from the root cellar—dark, damp, swallowing the air as soon as the door closed. The smell of wet earth pressed in, jars scraped against wooden shelves, your own breath echoing in the hollow dark, the glass cool against your fingertips. Every cousin feared it, but Gaylynn was sent most often. She never argued. She squared her shoulders, reluctantly walked into the chill, and came back with what was asked. In those moments she was learning, long before anyone noticed, how to walk straight through fear because there was no other way to reach the light. Even then, I believe God was already planting the seeds of endurance within her.

While Gaylynn was learning to steel herself against fear, my world looked very different. My house was steadier. My mother's quiet competence, my stepfather's patience, the nightly clatter of dishes—all gave me consistency. My stepfather, who had contracted polio during WWII and later relied on a wheelchair, refused to let disability be the headline of our lives. He cooked dinner, prayed over and with us, and taught me that love could be reliable. He showed me how to let my quiet confidence rise when it needed to, and reminded me that above all else, faith in God came first, followed closely by the importance of family. He adopted my older sister and me when we were very young, a defining act of permanence that gave me a sense of rootedness Gaylynn never had. My sister and I easily called him "dad."

Gaylynn's house was the opposite. Affection turned to anger in a heartbeat. She learned to read a room like a book—the set of a jaw, the slam of a glass, the silence that meant *stay out of sight*. She and her sister leaned on each other to endure, even as favoritism and unpredictability deepened their bond.

One night at their house seared itself into my memory. Dinner was simple—boiled hot dogs—but what unfolded was anything but. Gaylynn's younger sister, small and delicate from childhood illness, had developed a stutter that worsened under pressure. Their stepdad had a strict dinnertime rule: No one could leave the table until every bite was eaten. In a desperate attempt to avoid punishment, her sister stuffed the hot dog down her shirt, hoping no one would notice. Her stepdad, stretched out on the carpet, propped up on one elbow like a man sunbathing, called us over one by one, asking us questions like a detective on a mission. When it was her sister's turn, as she tried to step over him, the hot dog slipped from her shirt and landed squarely on him. She tried to quickly explain, but because of her stutter, she couldn't form the words fast enough. For a brief second, Gaylynn and I snickered, but her sister's face said it all: pure horror.

His rage erupted instantly. He sprang to his feet, screaming with a fury that seemed to shake the walls. As his hand rose to strike, Gaylynn stepped in and took the blow—hard across her face—along with the venomous words that followed. I froze, terrified, but she didn't. She shielded her sister, unflinchingly. That moment defined her in my mind: protective, brave, willing to bear pain so someone else wouldn't have to.

After what seemed like an eternity, her sister and I ran, slamming the door behind us and pressing our backs hard against the wall. The air in the room was thick with the smell of sweat and fear. When Gaylynn finally came in, her face was blotched red, streaked with tears, and unyielding all at once. We didn't have words for what was happening to us then; all we could do was cling to each other in silence, listening to our uneven breathing and the pounding of our hearts. Sleep came only in fragments, restless and shallow, but eventually it found us. At first light, our eyes met across the pillows, we held each other tightly, and never spoke of that night again.

I didn't tell my parents. I didn't have the language for it, and I didn't want to betray my cousin by dragging our secret into the light. After that, I made excuses to go home before dark. I still loved being with my cousins and going on another country adventure, but I tried to keep our time together in spaces where the sun could see us.

Other cruelties chipped away too: Work heaped unfairly. Praise withheld. A good day balanced on fragile whims. Gaylynn carried too much for a young girl: endless chores, the responsibility of protecting her younger sister, the constant expectation to endure.

And yet courage still found expression. It looked like going to the cellar. It looked like standing between her sister and a grown man's rage. It looked like believing, stubbornly, that light would find its way in.

We did have moments of cousin joy. Fourth of July sparklers traced our names in the night air. Porch swings groaned under our small, restless bodies. Sleepovers with popcorn and a box fan humming us into dreams gave us glimpses of softness.

One memory still makes me smile. Gaylynn's stepdad called her mother, screaming and demanding a calf be picked up immediately. The next thing I knew, the four of us—her mother, her sister, Gaylynn, and I—piled into her mother's tiny Volkswagen Bug and headed to the stockyard. Somehow, we wrangled that thing into the backseat of her mother's Bug. There we were—mom and sister in the front; me, Gaylynn, and the calf in the back. The poor, scared thing bawled as its hooves kept slipping on the vinyl seats, while we laughed until tears ran down our faces. Comedy collided with turmoil.

Even amid hardship, Gaylynn's gifts declared themselves. She was athletic, fast, strong—a natural on the softball diamond. Sports gave her rules she could trust: hit the ball, run; catch it, you're out. No shifting goalposts, no sudden eruptions. She thrived, and coaches noticed.

On the field she ran like she could outrun the past; in school activities she discovered small pockets of control and recognition. She also drew people to her with her quick wit and gift of gab—a natural people person.

I absorbed the contrasts. At her house, I learned which floorboards squeaked, how to fetch water without clattering ice. At mine, the sound of my father's cane and my mother's voice meant safety. It took me years to see it for what it was: Stability is wealth. Being loved without having to earn it—wealth beyond measure.

If it sounds like we lived two different childhoods, it's because we did. I had steadiness; she had turbulence. And yet, we were bound together as cousins, best friends, and products of very different houses. The contrast between our stepfathers said it all. My birth father left my mother before I was born, so I never knew him. My stepfather came into our lives when I was very young. He modeled faith, reliability, and quiet sacrifice. He wanted my sister and me to carry his name and feel a sense of belonging. Hers never did. Volatile and unpredictable, he left her learning how to brace for conflict. It was as though the men who entered our lives set the stage for the kind of safety—or uncertainty—we grew up expecting.

The contrast explains so much of what came later. It explains how Gaylynn could face the unthinkable—not without breaking, but with the will to piece herself back together each time. She had been practicing resilience all her life.

People sometimes ask how someone becomes the kind of woman who can face a surgeon's silence and not come undone. I can only point back here: to the cellar and the porch; to a grandmother whose love was as unpredictable as the weather; to a girl who was passed over yet chose to step forward anyway; to a softball field where running felt like self-determination and she seized every breath of it.

Before cancer, before unspeakable grief, there was a brave, bright girl with a stubborn will to live—shaped by hardship, yet still soft enough to love.

The worst of the unrest didn't arrive all at once. It unfolded slowly, like a road that seems straight until you hit the bend, and then it sharpens without warning. What once seemed like ordinary roughness was sharpening into something darker. The lessons of running, of reading rooms, of keeping your heart open—they would all be tested. The home that should have been her refuge became the place where wounds cut deepest. The unrest was no longer background noise; it was the air she breathed. And soon, it would demand more of her than any child should have to bear.

Two peas in a pod sharing the warmth of spring.
Their bond bright in the moment and tender in the keeping.

Me holding on to Gaylynn and the roots that held us together.

Behind the old wooden door, memories are stored like jars on a shelf.

Proof that not every childhood memory fits neatly in the backseat of an old car.

CHAPTER 2

FRACTURED FOUNDATIONS

*"What children live through in silence often becomes
the scaffolding of who they must become."*

Life at Gaylynn's house carried a rhythm all its own—sharp, uneven, and impossible to predict. What might start as an ordinary day could end in shouting, slammed doors, or the sudden announcement that everything was about to change. After spending time in the steadiness of my own home, stepping back into hers felt like walking across a floor where you never knew which boards would give way.

Gaylynn had already learned how to adapt. She held herself upright, refusing to let the unease around her bend her posture, her face unreadable, and her eyes quick to scan a room. While most children her age were still wrapped in the innocence of play, she was already learning how to measure danger by tone of voice, by footsteps on the porch, by the long silence before an argument exploded.

Her stepfather was at the center of much of that tension. His moods swung wide—sometimes playful, often domineering, always unpredictable. He liked control, and his threats to uproot the family became a steady backdrop. We're moving. I'll sell this place. Don't get comfortable. Those words were drilled into Gaylynn's childhood, keeping her and her younger sister off balance, never certain if the life they knew that week would survive to the next.

Even after they settled onto the forty-acre property, the threats didn't stop. The land might have promised consistency, but his words kept reminding them that nothing was permanent. The house creaked with more than age; it creaked with unease.

Gaylynn's mother didn't work outside the home, and her stepfather, before owning businesses, drove big trucks for a living. For years, their home life was one of financial struggle, but it was the emotional toll of his violent outbursts that truly marked their existence.

One day, after nearly a decade together with her stepfather, Gaylynn's mother became pregnant. A small flicker of hope ignited that the family might begin to settle, that joy could outweigh the turmoil. But tragedy struck. Gaylynn's stepfather came home in a rage, furious that Gaylynn, her younger sister, and their mother hadn't properly washed his eighteen-wheeler. His anger turned violent. He beat Gaylynn's mother so severely that she hemorrhaged and suffered a miscarriage.

When the frantic call came, my mother rushed over and drove my aunt to the hospital, while Gaylynn and her sister were left behind to clean the blood from the bathroom floor. Even then, in the middle of heartbreak no child should have witnessed, I believe God was there—grieving with them, even as His presence went unrecognized. The baby, a boy, was lost that day, his life ending before it had the chance to begin. The girls worked in silence broken only by soft, stifled sobs, their tears mixing with the water in the bucket. The sound of Gaylynn's sister wringing out bloody rags stayed with her for years—the rhythm of grief dressed as chores.

After that tragic event, Gaylynn doesn't recall any further physical abuse from her stepfather; however, the verbal abuse continued. Whether from guilt, fear of consequence, or simply a change in the family dynamic, the physical violence stopped—but the damage had already been done. The scars, though not always visible, ran deep, shaping Gaylynn's view of love, trust, and safety for years to come.

In time, her mother and stepfather welcomed two more children—a daughter and, later, a son. But as those children grew, Gaylynn began to see a clear divide in how the siblings were treated.

She and her younger sister remained responsible for all the house-work and farm chores, while the younger two were largely spared. The two younger children were allowed—and even encouraged—to participate in after-school activities, attend social events, and spend time with friends, privileges Gaylynn and her sister were rarely, if ever, afforded.

The cruelty went further. Her younger half siblings would often mock Gaylynn and her sister while they worked, laughing as the older girls carried the brunt of the family's labor. Their laughter was sharp, cutting through the summer air as the girls bent to weed rows of vegetables or haul buckets of water. It was a constant reminder that, in their stepfather's eyes, Gaylynn and her sister were never truly "his" children. That difference, along with the abuse, shaped everything.

School was no refuge. In their household, education never carried the weight that work and obedience did. For Gaylynn, classrooms became less about learning and more about endurance—another place to get through until she could escape to the fields or onto the ball diamond, where the rules at least made sense.

The daily grind was unrelenting. Work piled high, often more than any child should have carried. Chores extended far beyond tidying up or helping with dinner. Gaylynn was mowing acres of grass, hauling buckets of animal feed, washing not only the family car but the semitrucks her stepfather drove for work. Delicate from child-hood illness, her sister, who was only a child herself, was not shielded from labor. She was expected to pitch in—trimming grass along the fencerow with scissors, her small hands struggling to keep up. The tasks were endless, the standard was ever changing like a moving target. When she couldn't complete the tasks, without a word, Gaylynn absorbed what was left, usually most of it. Praise rarely came her way. If her sister faltered, Gaylynn was expected to pick up the slack. If Gaylynn excelled, it was brushed aside, as though effort and achievement were simply her duty.

And yet, she endured.

One summer afternoon, I was invited to join the girls for a day of fun, but only after they finished their "yard work." I imagined sweeping the porch, maybe watering flowers. Instead, a list scrawled in thick black pen covered half the kitchen table: mow, weed, trim, haul, sweep. By the time they finished—sweat stinging their eyes and dirt caked under their nails—her stepfather added more: washing the semis, polishing chrome until the rags shredded to threads. The sun slid lower, shadows lengthened, but still the work went on. He wouldn't let me help because, as he put it, he was "teaching them a lesson." What that lesson was, I never knew.

That was the rhythm of life in Gaylynn's house. Enough was never enough.

The atmosphere inside the farmhouse was no kinder. A slammed cabinet, a door shut a little too hard, the wrong answer to a question asked in the wrong tone—any of it could ignite his fury. Gaylynn's mother tried to hold the family together, but her exhaustion and fear bled through. The girls lived under a constant cloud of tension, never knowing when the next outburst would come.

Gaylynn grew adept at reading the weather of her home. She could sense when to disappear, when to keep her sister close, when to stand her ground. It wasn't the kind of skill any child should have to learn, but it became second nature. Each confrontation, each cruel word, each unpredictable swing of mood pressed her deeper into a resilience she shouldn't have had to summon so young.

By the time we reached our early teens, I noticed how different our worlds truly were. In my house, steadiness came almost without effort; in hers, peace was always precarious, and nightfall often meant knots in the stomach, bracing for conflict.

Gaylynn's childhood home was no sanctuary. It was a crucible. And like all crucibles, it was shaping her—sometimes through love, but far more often through fire.

With the perspective of time, these years laid the groundwork for the woman she would become. Every unpredictable turn taught her how to adapt. Every slammed door taught her how to brace without breaking. Every injustice carved a determination not to be undone.

The worst of the upheaval didn't descend all at once. It gathered layer upon layer until darkness felt like the air she breathed. And yet within that dimness, something was forming. The girl who had been forced to shoulder more than her share was beginning to discover sparks of power that no one could take from her.

Soon, those sparks would find expression—in school, in sports, and in every space where she could carve out a sense of self. The home that tried to control her would not have the final say. Yet the burdens around her life were far from lifting. What had begun as turbulence inside four walls was seeping outward, the pressure tightening with each passing year.

What Gaylynn carried was more than bruises.

CHAPTER 3

FINDING HER VOICE

*"Strength born of survival has a way
of sounding louder than fear."*

Gaylynn had moments of awkwardness in her early teens, but even then, there was something undeniably captivating about her. She carried herself with a natural confidence, and her quick-witted sense of humor developed early on. She had a way of commanding attention—not intentionally or boastfully, but simply because her energy was magnetic. The moment she walked into a room, she had the ability to make people laugh, a trait she inherited from her mother. Her presence filled the space like a bright light cutting through darkness. No one could resist being drawn to her, and even at such a young age, she instinctively understood the power of making others feel seen and valued. It wasn't just about being the center of attention; it was about finding joy in making people feel better in their own skin.

I, on the other hand, was the complete opposite. Quiet, shy, and withdrawn, I kept to myself, rarely speaking to anyone outside my family. In school, I didn't speak a word—not even to teachers—until sixth grade. Today, I might have been labeled a selective mute, but back then, labels weren't often used for children who were different. My teachers were concerned, of course—but not my parents. They simply smiled when the concerns were shared with them, saying, "She's fine. She talks all the time at home." And they were right. At home, I was a chatterbox. Being the youngest in my blended family, I would often boss everyone else around, get my way by any means possible, and developed a strong, independent personality early. But outside of that safe space, I was unsure of how to find my voice. In public, with so many siblings ready to speak for me, I often chose silence.

While I eventually grew into my own quiet confidence, it didn't happen at the same pace as Gaylynn's. She had a natural ease about her—an energy that was infectious, an assurance that seemed indestructible. From my perspective, no matter what life threw at her, she adapted, persisted, and often used humor to shield herself from the conflict around her. I now realize her boldness was more than simply a personality trait; it was born out of endurance. In navigating her sometimes cruel and unpredictable world, humor and charm were both armor and escape. Where I could afford to be reserved, she had no choice but to be bold. Where I could take my time finding my voice, she had to use hers early and often. Her confidence wasn't simply who she was; it was a defense mechanism, a way to endure.

By the time Gaylynn entered her teenage years, something inside her had begun to transform. She was no longer the little girl navigating a world of abuse, volatility, and unpredictability; she was becoming someone who could find the faintest spark in a cavern of despair. The contrast between our lives sharpened as we grew, but what struck me most was how Gaylynn kept finding ways to rise, even when the heaviness pressing down on her should have kept her from standing.

At the heart of this resilience was the bond she shared with her younger sister. From the time they were small, they had never been far apart—thick as thieves, bound together in a way only sisters can be. But more than sisters, they were each other's lifeline. When tempers flared, they huddled together. When chores piled high, they turned the work into teamwork, tossing jokes back and forth or daring each other into small rebellions that made the labor bearable. When fear crept in, they leaned on each other with an unspoken wordless trust, the kind forged only in households where staying safe comes first.

Their bond was undeniable and unshakable. The sisters rarely slept alone at night; they were always together. And after their stepfather's yelling subsided, the two of them spoke in hushed tones until sleep finally claimed them. Looking back now, I see how God used their quiet promises and shared resilience as a kind of shield, holding them together when nothing else in that house did. In the mornings, they faced each day side by side, presenting a united front even when they were delicate inside. The sister's health issues made her physically more vulnerable, and Gaylynn carried that responsibility like armor, as protection for her sister.

Most children spend their early years carefree, worrying about little more than scraped knees or math homework. For Gaylynn, the stakes were higher. She was learning, day by day, how to read danger before it arrived, how to keep her sister safe, how to bend without breaking. She may have seemed like the stronger one, but in truth, they held each other up. That bond was their steady rhythm when the world around them refused to stay steady.

Even as she leaned on her bond with her sister, Gaylynn was carving out space for herself. By her teens, the softball field had become more than an escape; it was where she turned the volatility of home into drive. Coaches began to notice her speed and her instinct for leadership, calling her name with a recognition she rarely heard inside her own house. Yet even in the middle of victories, part of her mind stayed tethered to her younger sister. Success never erased the question that shadowed her steps: Was her sister safe at home without her?

Besides success in athletics, Gaylynn's magnetic personality made her stand out at school. Tall and lean, with quick humor and easy to converse with, she carried herself with a confidence that masked the unrest she returned to each night. Classmates gravitated toward her, drawn to the way she could make them laugh or rally them around a project. If the house she grew up in made her feel invisible, the wider world reminded her she could be seen.

Around that time, my life was changing too. I married while Gaylynn was still in high school, and she stood with me on that day—bright, steady, wholly present, though tears slipped quietly down her cheeks. I didn't understand it then, but later she told me my wedding was also one of the worst days of her life. Because my husband and I were moving away, Gaylynn felt as if I were leaving her behind—and I was the one person with whom she always felt safe. Her honesty revealed the depth of our bond and how hard distance would be for her heart. In time I came to see that her sense of safety with me had been shaped by the instability of her home; my leaving felt like one more piece of solid ground giving way. Yet when I look back at the photographs, our smiles tell a different story—mirroring one another with the kind of joy only years of shared history can hold.

While she was in high school, a modeling agent took notice of her, offering her work in local bridal shows. Flattered, she saw this as a way to earn money and escape the house. But the agent had one condition: She had to cut her hair. He explained that to properly showcase the back of the bridal gowns, her long, dark locks had to go. Gaylynn agreed, and the stylist's scissors fell heavy as they trimmed away what had always been her signature look. Within what felt like minutes, her long, flowing dark hair was being swept up off the floor.

When she returned home, she was excited to show off her new hairstyle. Her mother's reaction, however, was immediate and violent. Shocked and furious, she grabbed Gaylynn by the hair on the back of her head, yanked her to the ground, slapped her across the face, and screamed at her. Confused and frightened, Gaylynn simply apologized again and again. In hindsight, she came to understand that her mother's outburst wasn't about the haircut; it was about control. For years, her mother had brushed and combed Gaylynn's long hair, and watching her daughter make such a decision without permission felt like rebellion and betrayal. Cutting her hair, for Gaylynn, was an act of independence. I believe those moments of defiance—painful as they were—were also glimpses of a deeper resolve God was shaping in her, a strength she would one day lean on when the stakes were far greater.

Not long after, Gaylynn stepped more fully into modeling. It might seem like a contradiction—sports on one hand, posing in front of cameras on the other—but for her, both aspects of her life were connected. Modeling gave her another stage, another chance to be noticed for something beyond the struggles at home. She loved the way the lights felt warm on her skin, how slipping into a dress or carefully styled outfit transformed her reflection. The click of the camera shutter echoed like a promise: She could exist in another story, another frame—one she chose.

We were cousins and best friends, but Gaylynn and her sister were partners in endurance. That bond was one I could never fully touch, because my life simply didn't require it. As Gaylynn found her voice, I could see how much of it came from that very bond. She was bold because she had to be. She was resilient because she refused to let her sister face life by herself. The courage she carried onto the softball field, the modeling stage, the classroom—that courage had been trained in the late-night stories, the shared burdens, the wordless agreement between sisters that neither of them would face the darkness alone.

Throughout high school, Gaylynn was becoming someone larger than the confines of her house. But burdens don't vanish just because the spotlight shines. The bond with her sister, enduring as it seemed, was also delicate in ways none of us understood then. It carried too much responsibility, too many demands, too many secrets. And though their bond carried them through childhood and well into adulthood, strains were already forming beneath the surface.

For now, though, Gaylynn was finding her voice. She was running bases with a fire in her chest, stepping in front of cameras with a glint in her eye, and standing in the mirror with hair cut on her own terms. She was learning what it meant to be visible.

But even as she stepped forward, the unrest at home never loosened its grip. The tension lingered like weather building on the horizon. Her confidence and independence were real, but so was the darkness pressing in behind her.

What none of us knew then was how deeply that darkness would test her—and how even the strongest bonds could bend beneath the pressure of life.

My wedding with Gaylynn by my side and our bond that never faded.

CHAPTER 4

THROUGH THE ASHES

"Even the smallest ember can carry the memory of fire."

True to her independent and strong-willed nature, Gaylynn moved out of her parents' home at just seventeen. She had endured enough of the turmoil and dysfunction that had marked her childhood, and by that age she was determined to create her own path. With a stubborn resilience that had become her trademark, she rented a small apartment and began carving out a life on her own terms. For the first time, she had a key that opened her own door, furniture that belonged to her, and a refrigerator she stocked herself. Those little things mattered; they were symbols of independence, a sign she refused to be confined.

During this time, she was dating her first serious boyfriend, who would soon become her husband. Their relationship progressed quickly, too quickly. By twenty, Gaylynn was married, and the couple purchased a house together. She filled the rooms with touches that reflected her desire for the warmth of a loving home: soft curtains, framed photographs, flowers picked fresh from the yard. She hung pictures in the hallway and made plans for holiday dinners, imagining the kind of family life she had always longed for as a girl. From the outside, this hopeful beginning appeared to be the picture of young adulthood unfolding just as it should.

But behind closed doors, the story was very different. The marriage unraveled almost from the start. Drugs crept in—first casually, then persistently. A pill on the weekend became a nightly habit. What began as occasional experimentation spiraled into dependency. The air inside their home grew thick, heavy with tension as the abuse escalated. Arguments erupted out of nothing—accusations, slammed doors, apologies that came too late or not at all. Gaylynn knew the rhythm of dysfunction: the rush of excitement when he was affectionate, the crash of betrayal when he wasn't.

Infidelity surfaced too, a betrayal that cut deep. She discovered phone calls she wasn't meant to hear, saw signs of another life carried out in secret. Each discovery chipped away at her trust until the foundation of their marriage crumbled. At night she lay awake, staring at the ceiling, asking herself how she had ended up in another prison. She had run from the insecurity of her childhood only to find herself right back in it, this time bound by vows and a shared mortgage.

After two painful years, the marriage ended. The divorce papers were a strange relief—an ending laced with grief but also release.

During this turbulent time, Gaylynn began her own descent into substance abuse. Drugs became her way of coping, a shield against the heartbreak. A few hours of haze dulled the sharp edges of her pain, but it was never enough. When the fog lifted, the reality of her broken marriage returned heavier than before. This cycle followed her for years, a darkness that clung to her even as she fought for new beginnings.

After her first divorce, Gaylynn didn't remain alone for long. She met someone new, and their connection was immediate. Once again, her desire for love and belonging pulled her in quickly, and soon they had moved to Chicago. The big city was a stark contrast to the hometown she had known. Neon lights blinked late into the night, the sound of traffic hummed constantly, and the anonymity of crowds made her feel invisible in both freeing and frightening ways.

For a while, the city felt like an escape. She loved the rhythm of its streets, the way she could walk into a store and not recognize a single face. Chicago meant possibility: new restaurants, music, adventures that stretched late into the night. She felt briefly like a new person, untethered from her past. But the fractures came quickly. The relationship, like her marriage before it, soured with familiar patterns of infidelity and mistrust. The excitement of the city dimmed, replaced by loneliness. Instead of freedom, the crowds became suffocating.

When the relationship ended, she found herself stranded—emotionally depleted and financially broke. Pride gave way to necessity, and she called her parents for help. Her stepfather bought her a ticket home. She boarded the plane, her spirit worn thin, her bag heavy not only with clothes but with disappointment.

Not long after returning, Gaylynn discovered she was pregnant.

The news came like a wave. She was already exhausted from the upheavals of recent years, and yet inside her was the delicate beginning of new life. She was terrified, but also quietly hopeful. Shortly after, she met a man who surprised her. Despite knowing about the pregnancy, he loved her anyway. He was kind, attentive, and steady in a way that made her feel secure. He held her hand through morning sickness, reassured her with promises of stability, and made her believe that maybe, just maybe, this time would be different.

For a few months, life steadied. His support softened the fear, allowing her to imagine a future where she wasn't alone.

But about six months into the pregnancy, Gaylynn began to feel unwell. Her complexion grew pale, her energy drained. One afternoon, by chance, she ran into her first husband. He stopped, concern flashing across his face. "You look gray," he told her bluntly. "Most pregnant women glow." She quickly made a joke about his comments and tried to brush off the seriousness of his tone. But the words haunted her, clinging like a warning.

She kept examining herself in the mirror, hoping she would see the glow of an expectant mother. The reflection looking back at her was anything but radiant. She scheduled a visit with her doctor. The room carried that scrubbed, clinical chill as the Doppler moved across her belly. She held her breath, waiting for the reassuring rhythm of a heartbeat. But the room stayed quiet. The doctor searched, tried again, and then delivered the devastating news: There was no heartbeat.

Her baby had died.

Because she was into her second trimester, she would have to deliver her stillborn child.

I was there in the hospital room with her. I will never forget the hours that followed. The room was cold, filled with the steady beeping of machines and the quiet shuffle of nurses coming and going. Gaylynn lay in bed, her body wracked with contractions, knowing the outcome would not be a cry . . . but silence. I held her hand and prayed as she endured wave after wave of pain. The nurses moved softly in and out, their voices low, their eyes filled with sympathy, carrying a sorrow words could not express. Minutes stretched into hours, each one heavy with agony. And still, I prayed.

When it was finally over, she delivered a stillborn baby girl. She named her *Star*.

The name was perfect—something bright and beautiful, but fleeting. She never had the chance to hold her, to see her eyes, to hear her cry. Star's life began and ended in silence.

The moment left an indelible mark. For Gaylynn, the loss was a grief too deep to put into words. For me, I felt the helplessness of watching someone I loved walk through a fire I could not quench. I already had a family of my own, and while I could empathize, I knew I could never fully grasp the depth of her loss. Unless you've stood in that place, no one can. All I could do was sit with her in the darkness, listen when she could speak, and pray when she couldn't.

Later, Gaylynn told me what it felt like to lie in that hospital bed afterward. All around her, life bloomed. Mothers laughed, babies cried, families celebrated in nearby rooms. The sound of joy seeped under the door, each laugh and cry a dagger in her heart. It was a cruel contrast—her loss against their gain. Understandably, she fell into deep depression. It was the first time I saw her overtaken by a heaviness that seemed immovable.

Despite the loss, she stayed with the man who had supported her through the pregnancy. Eventually, they became engaged. For a time, she tried to rebuild hope, but the gaps soon appeared. Not long after announcing their engagement, she became pregnant again. This time, when she told him, his reaction was chilling. He was angry and demanded she get rid of "it."

Conflicted and emotionally worn down, she complied. The memory of Star was still raw, Gaylynn's self-worth eroded by grief and exhaustion. She silenced her instincts in order to keep the peace, to hold on to the semblance of steadiness.

A few months later, she found herself pregnant again. Once more, he insisted she end the pregnancy. Again, she complied. Each time she gave in to his demand, it chipped away at her spirit, deepening wounds that never had time to heal. Complying with controlling men was a lesson she had absorbed from her mother, and though she hated herself for it, defiance felt impossible.

After the second abortion, something in Gaylynn shifted. Suspicion grew. His absences, his excuses, the distance in his tone—all of it pointed to betrayal, a feeling she knew all too well. She decided to follow him.

Her heart pounded as she trailed his car, her hands gripping the wheel tightly. Every turn confirmed what she already feared. When she arrived at another woman's house, the truth was undeniable. He was inside.

The infidelity ignited a rage she had kept buried for too long. Fueled by grief and heartbreak, she broke into the woman's home and found them together. The confrontation exploded. Years of loss, pain, and betrayal poured out of her fists. The fury that had been bottled inside erupted with terrifying force. By the time it was over, he was in the emergency room.

The relationship with the man who had once been so kind to her in the beginning, who had walked her through the miscarriage of Star, and demanded she abort two pregnancies ended immediately after this explosion. This was another chapter marked by devastation, but also a turning point. For the first time, she had unleashed the fire inside her rather than swallowing it.

She had walked through burning coals, carrying the ashes of broken dreams, and though the flames threatened to consume her, she emerged changed. Scarred, yes, but stronger.

Through the ashes, Gaylynn began to realize that her voice, her choices, and her power belonged to her alone. The world could wound her, but it would not tame her.

CHAPTER 5

SEARCHING FOR SHELTER

"Somewhere in the storm, a quiet voice whispers, hold on." — Anonymous

Gaylynn's parents lived in a rhythm of extremes—seasons of feast followed by famine, stretches of abundance that gave way to sudden scarcity. Money would appear, only to vanish with equal speed, leaving bills unpaid and the lights threatening to go dark. Just when Gaylynn thought security had finally arrived, it slipped away again. That cycle, so familiar to her as a child, followed her as she grew into a young woman.

By the time Gaylynn was in her late twenties, after the volatile end of her engagement to the man who had demanded the abortions, her life had moved into a rhythm that was both full and precarious. She began a family with the man who would become her second husband, before they were wed. By the time they took their vows, their family was already complete: three daughters with quick smiles and bright eyes, binding Gaylynn to a life of monumental responsibility. Marriage was less a beginning and more a formality stamped onto years of shared family ties.

While raising three little girls, very close in age—her entire heart wrapped in tiny hands and the pitter-patter of little feet—she was tethered to a relationship that often felt more like an anchor than a lifeline. Her second husband was in and out of the picture in the early days of their young family. He could be affectionate and charming, but more often he was absent—sometimes emotionally, sometimes physically—leaving Gaylynn to bear the burden of motherhood on her own.

Her sister remained her closest ally during those years. The two of them had already weathered so much together. That bond gave Gaylynn the will to endure, even as cracks began to form under the pressure of too much responsibility.

Peace of mind was elusive. The only housing Gaylynn and her family could afford was in a shady part of town—a building that had once been a soup kitchen for the homeless. I couldn't help but notice the irony. A place where the hungry had once been fed now became the walls that sheltered her young family. It felt, in its own way, like a quiet provision—God turning ruins into refuge.

The sign was gone, but its reputation remained. Strangers still knocked on their door, hoping for a hot meal or a place to rest—sometimes a weary man smelling of alcohol, other times a gaunt woman clutching a paper bag as if it held her whole life. Gaylynn refused to open the door, but she never forgot the sound of the knocking either; it carried the echo of desperation that mirrored her own fear of never being able to give her girls more than scraps.

The neighborhood was as rough as the building itself. Broken bottles glittered like sharp confetti along the sidewalks, and the sound of sirens was as common as birdsong. She refused to let her daughters play in the front yard, steering them instead to remain inside the house where her watchful eye could guard against the constant shuffle of strangers. In that cramped space, she created a fortress out of almost nothing: plastic toys stacked in corners, a swing rigged inside with worn ropes, the clean scent of hand-me-down clothes washed and hung to dry across the room.

Finances were tight, and she stretched every dollar, sometimes skipping meals herself to make sure her girls had enough to eat. Pride kept her from admitting it to anyone, but later she confessed how often she felt overwhelmed by the fear of not being able to provide.

Somehow, the girls always had enough—evidence of a God who provides, even when His hand goes unnoticed in the moment.

Raising three daughters almost on her own was no easy feat. Gaylynn worked tirelessly, often juggling multiple jobs just to keep food on the table and a roof over their heads. There were stretches when she barely slept, pushing through sheer exhaustion—not because she wanted to, but because she had no other choice.

Her husband's presence was uncertain, flickering in and out like a light bulb with loose wiring. When he was there, he was often distracted, absent in the ways that mattered most. Arguments sparked easily, the air in the small home tightening with words unsaid and resentments unhealed. Separation came, then reunion, then the cycle began again. She often feared that the girls were learning early to feel the tension in their parents' marriage before words were even spoken—the same way she had once learned to read the shifting moods of her own childhood home. But she didn't know then how to break that cycle. And so, it continued.

And yet, through it all, she held on. She found ways to soften the hardness: Warm baths scented with dollar-store soap that smelled faintly of lilacs. Little touches of normalcy that told her daughters they were safe, even if the world outside their door was not.

During this season of hardship, something unexpected began to stir in her. While most saw only her circumstances, she started to see possibilities. The very walls around her—the shelter-turned-home—planted a seed of curiosity. Buildings told stories. Houses carried meaning. If she could ever step beyond barely getting by, perhaps real estate could be more than a roof over her head. Perhaps it could be a path.

Her interest in real estate began as curiosity, but it grew into determination. She started by watching friends and acquaintances navigate the market, drawn to the energy of the business and the possibilities she imagined for herself. Her charisma, people skills, and sharp instincts seemed a natural fit. After the girls were tucked into bed and the house finally quieted, Gaylynn often sat at the kitchen table under the dim glow of a worn lamp, stacks of books spread before her. Financing terms, property law, escrow accounts—the material wasn't easy to absorb, but she pressed through each page with the same tenacity she had once used to push through endless chores on the farm.

Some nights she doubted herself, wondering if she had stepped too far outside her reach. Yet something in her spirit told her to keep going. She wasn't just studying for a license; she was studying for a future, for a chance to give her girls the steady footing she had never known.

When she finally passed the Realtor exam, it wasn't just a credential. It was a victory, a declaration that she could step into a new world on her own terms.

Her first listing came not long after, and she poured herself into it. She staged and polished every detail until she was certain the home would shine. The day she hammered her first "For Sale" sign into the ground, she stood back and let herself feel the significance of it. That simple wooden post, with its bright placard swinging in the breeze, symbolized far more than a house on the market. For her, it was proof she had taken the first step toward rewriting her story.

The pride only deepened when she signed her first contract and received her first commission check. She held it in her hands, almost disbelieving that this new path could bring such reward. This path was about more than money; it was about the dignity of building something through her own determination. She also discovered a deep joy in helping others realize their dream of owning a home. Even then, she was finding ways to put others first.

For a time, the business seemed to promise a steady climb. Each sale added to her confidence, proof that she had carved out a future on her own terms. But money, as it always had, carried its own tension. In the lean months, when deals were slow and bills stacked up, the atmosphere between her and her husband grew heavy. Arguments sharpened, words edged with fear of not having enough. Finger-pointing became a language of its own, as if blame could fill the empty spaces in their bank account.

In contrast, when sales picked up and commissions flowed in, the mood shifted. Trips were planned, smiles came easier, and for a while the fractures in their marriage seemed to smooth over. It was a pattern familiar to Gaylynn—feast followed by famine—but this time, she was no longer just enduring it. She was beginning to see a way forward, learning how to turn unreliability into momentum.

They moved the girls out of the former homeless shelter and into an older home in the city. The place had character—scuffed base-boards, windows that rattled a little when the wind blew—but it was theirs. The scent of fresh paint still lingered from Gaylynn's touch-ups, and she planted flowers by the front steps so the girls would see color greeting them when they came home. It wasn't perfect, but it was safe, and to Gaylynn that made it beautiful. That move was a change of address but also proof that persistence could open new doors, and it fueled Gaylynn's determination to keep reaching for more.

Even with the new stability, Gaylynn never forgot their humble beginnings in the former soup kitchen. She remembered the strag-glers who would knock on the door, and her heart ached for them. Out of that memory, she began a tradition with her girls: On major holidays, instead of focusing on decorations or gifts, they volunteered together at the current soup kitchens or shelters. She wanted her daughters to carry forward compassion and never forget where they had once been.

Gaylynn had never known a time when she wasn't working. From a young age, she was taught—often through harsh and unreason-able demands—that hard work was not optional. She attributes her tireless hustle to her stepfather's relentless insistence that she carry more than her share of responsibility, even as a child. Though born of hardship, that early conditioning had shaped a determination that has served her well throughout her life.

Always striving to move forward, she launched and managed her own property management company, juggling multiple ventures with relentless energy and focus. She earned a reputation not only for her business savvy but for her dedication and drive. In the highly competitive world of real estate, she thrived, proving not only to others but to herself that she was capable of standing tall and succeeding on her own terms.

The rhythm of rise and fall had followed her into adulthood, but she managed it differently than her parents had. She refused to let her daughters feel the depth of uncertainty she once knew.

The lessons of her childhood carried Gaylynn through those years. She was resourceful, quick to adapt, always looking for a backup plan. Her determination became her daughters' safety net, just as faith in God—however tentative in those days—was becoming hers. When I think back to Gaylynn in those years, I don't see only the hardships, though they were many. I see her durability taking shape, her spirit hardening and softening at the same time. She was still learning, still stumbling, still falling short in places . . . but she was also beginning to rise.

She couldn't have known then what losses still waited down the road: grief deeper than what she had already endured, battles fiercer than any she had fought yet. But she also couldn't have known the triumphs—that the young woman who once lived in a former soup kitchen would one day enter rooms where people saw her as a leader, where her voice would be significant, where her story would inspire others to hold on.

I see those years as the bridge between Gaylynn's endurance and her toughness. Childhood had forced her to adapt. Young adulthood taught her how to fight for security, even when it slipped through her fingers. And though she could not have known it then, these very struggles were preparing her for the greatest battle of her life.

Because one day, decades later, she would sit in a hospital room, hearing the words no one is ever ready to hear: stage 4 colon cancer. And when that day came, she would reach for the same grit, the same resourcefulness, the same unyielding will she had carried since she was a child. The fight for security had always been her fight. Cancer was simply another trial—more formidable, darker, but one she had unknowingly been preparing to face all along.

At the time, she was doing what she could with what she had, in a world that gave little and demanded much. Searching for shelter not only in walls and roofs, but in faith, in love for her girls, and in the stubborn belief that somewhere in the turmoil, a quiet voice was still telling her: Hold on.

SHADOWS AND TRIALS

"When you pass through the waters, I will be with you; and when you pass through the rivers, they will not sweep over you."— Isaiah 43:2

Grief has a sound. It doesn't always arrive with wailing or sobs; sometimes it's quieter—like the steady drip of rain seeping through a roof you thought would hold. It carries a heaviness, pressing into the chest, slowing every breath. By the time Gaylynn was lying on that operating table years later, bracing for cancer surgery, she already knew that burden. She had carried it long before doctors ever spoke the word tumor.

She has always had a way of cutting through the heaviness with humor. Even in the middle of her struggles, she'd call or text me with: *Can you get on the Batphone to God for me?* Half joke, half prayer, it was pure Gaylynn—raw, unfiltered, refusing to let despair have the last word. That phrase always made me laugh, even when the situation was anything but funny. But beneath the humor was something deeper: her stubborn desire to believe God was listening, and her unspoken confidence that I would be persistent enough to keep calling on Him. It was her way of admitting she needed prayer without ever giving up her grit.

I can still picture it—her stance steady, her smile offered freely to the world. Yet behind her eyes lived a weight she never fully outran. She could light up a room with humor, disarm strangers with warmth, but if you looked long enough, you saw the shadow. Grief never really leaves; it only changes form.

Her childhood had prepared her for slammed doors, unpredictable moods, the kind of fear you measure in footsteps and silence. But the hardships that came later were different. They weren't tempers you could dodge or tempests you could wait out. They were shattering. They broke through the walls she had built, sweeping away the fragile safety she had pieced together.

I won't name those losses yet. To do so would be to rush the storm, to strip it of its slow approach—the gathering clouds, the first distant thunder. What I will say is this: When these losses came, they demanded everything of her. And they left marks deeper than any visible wound.

That is the Gaylynn who was wheeled into the OR years later. Not a woman untouched by pain, but one remade by it. Not naive to loss, but already intimate with it. And yet: still standing, still fighting, still daring to believe that life could be lived, even in the shadows.

To grasp how she faced the surgeon's silence, you first have to know the trials that came before—the ones that stripped her bare yet taught her to plant her feet even when the ground beneath her gave way. What none of us could see then was that God was already equipping her, not only to endure, but to stand with a strength that would one day steady others too.

CHAPTER 6

SHIFTING BONDS

"The hardest storms aren't always the ones outside your window." — Anonymous

Just as life seemed to be settling, another fracture split through the family. Gaylynn's half sister had been living in a violent relationship, one that left her bruised and broken but still tethered by fear and dependence. The abuse had gone on for years, and everyone carried a quiet dread, waiting for the day it might finally take her life.

One afternoon, after another brutal beating, she picked up the phone and called their parents. Her voice shook as she pleaded for help, saying she couldn't endure it any longer. The call was raw, desperate—a daughter reaching back for the safety she had barely known, asking the only people she thought could save her. For Gaylynn, hearing about it was another reminder of how destructive family patterns can be. Pain from childhood hadn't disappeared; it had grown new branches, spreading into the next generation.

I can only imagine how that call echoed through Gaylynn's family. When my mother heard, she must have also felt an ache of both familiarity and helplessness, a reminder of nights spent holding her own sister through bruises and broken promises, wondering if anything would ever change.

Determined to intervene, Gaylynn's mother and stepfather—her half sister's biological father—went to get her out. As her stepfather approached the front door, the abuser threw it open and kicked him in the middle of his chest, sending him flying backward onto the concrete sidewalk. He hit hard and lay unconscious. What followed was horrific. The man began kicking and beating him as he lay helpless, stopping only when police arrived and arrested him.

Gaylynn's stepfather was rushed to the hospital and admitted to the ICU, clinging to life. Machines hummed and monitors glowed, their steady beeps a cruel reminder of how fragile he had become. As his condition worsened, he was transferred to a larger facility for more advanced care. When Gaylynn's younger sister called to say it didn't look good, her husband insisted Gaylynn go and be with the family. She, along with the others, grappled with the trauma of seeing the man who had once inflicted so much harm now lying broken and fragile.

The weeks that followed were chaotic. Gaylynn's half sister swung between declaring she was done with her abuser and then, in tears, finding her way back into his orbit—even while he was behind bars. There were late-night calls, promises made and broken. The family tried to help but were caught in the cycle of rescue and relapse. For Gaylynn, the drama was painful to watch—a mirror of her own memories of trying to hold steady in a home that never truly was.

Despite the medical team's best efforts, the monitors told the truth before the doctors said it aloud: His injuries were too severe. The family gathered at the hospital when he passed away, tangled in pain, history, and complicated grief. For Gaylynn, he had been both provider and oppressor. His expectations had been harsh, his presence domineering. She carried scars from his rule, but his death was not something she could easily shrug off. It forced open doors she had worked hard to close.

It was strange to stand at the edge of his life, remembering the man who had once broken her spirit, now broken himself in such a tragic way. Yet, in the years before his death, he had softened into a different role: a doting grandfather offering the kind of warmth and attention Gaylynn had rarely received herself. For all the pain he had caused her, Gaylynn felt torn watching him become someone her children loved and admired. The contrast between the man she had endured and the man her daughters adored left her with complex emotions she could not easily sort.

The morning of the funeral arrived gray, tight, and windy. Clouds hung low enough to touch, and the light in them was flat, as if they couldn't decide whether to pour down rain. People gathered in small clusters near the church doors, voices low, hands wrapped around stiff paper programs. Inside, the air carried the old scent of polish and hymnals, mixed with the sweetness of flowers set too close together. The casket at the front was heavy, as if memory itself had weight. White lilies spilled their fragrance into the room, sharp and insistent, a sweetness at odds with the heartache in the pews.

I watched Gaylynn take her place with the family. She stood straight, chin lifted just enough to say she would not be undone in public. She has always known how to carry herself when the ground buckles; that steadiness was learned. The priest began with words meant to comfort. At times they did; other times, they skimmed across the surface. A hymn followed—voices searching for the same note, then finding it together. I didn't sing. I listened to the shuffle of paper, the rustle of coats, the cough that kept interrupting from the aisle. Grief spread like a shadow through the room, touching everyone differently.

When the tears came, they came fast and unguarded. Gaylynn blinked through them, breath uneven, her gaze fixed just past the flowers. Later she admitted she wasn't sure what she was mourning— the man himself, the childhood she never had, or the years spent learning how to be small. Loss rarely fits a neat category. The eulogy tried to gather a life into one arc, but I heard the tug-of-war between stories safe to share at the pulpit and those that stayed in the corners, unspoken but heavy.

Gaylynn's half sister sat at the front of the church with their mother, rocking back and forth, her wailing so loud it drowned out the priest's words. It jarred against the stillness of the room. Part of me wanted to recoil: How could she cry so freely when so much of this might have been avoided? Yet even as I bristled, I recognized she too was caught in the cycle of abuse that had shaped their mother's life. The scene was perplexing but softened by understanding: Her grief, however misplaced it seemed, was real.

We followed the hearse to the cemetery, a slow line of cars under trees that had seen more farewells than any of us would. The wind snapped at coats, leaves skittered across the path, and the earth lay freshly opened, waiting. A final prayer rose into the air. Small gestures cut through the formality: a cousin reaching for another's hand, and that cousin not letting go. Contradictions filled the moment—ritual offering closure, memory refusing it.

When it was over, people lingered awkwardly, unsure whether to leave. I hugged Gaylynn, and she clung to me as if she would never let go. Others offered simple words—"I'm sorry for your loss"—that never reach as far as they mean to. The sky brightened but never cleared. That felt right for the day. Driving home, I watched the landscape slip past and thought how endings rarely end anything. They simply reopen rooms we thought we had locked.

Anguish didn't end at the cemetery; it trailed them into courtrooms and verdicts that brought little peace. When we heard he'd been charged and convicted of manslaughter for the attack, it felt, for a fleeting moment, like justice had arrived. But it didn't last. His sentence was reduced to involuntary manslaughter, and with time he walked free again. What shocked the rest of us most was not the legal outcome but Gaylynn's half sister's choices. She visited him faithfully in prison, eventually marrying him there and even bringing two children into the world while he was still behind bars. When he was released, she returned to him as though nothing had changed, and the cycle of abuse began again. Watching it unfold was disorienting, like seeing someone walk back into a burning house. For Gaylynn, her half sister's actions were beyond comprehension, a decision that deepened the wound already cut wide by their stepfather's death.

This tragedy widened the distance between the sisters. Gaylynn told her half sister she wanted nothing to do with her and would not allow her to be around her children. For a time, she allowed her half sister's older son from a previous relationship to stay with her, but even then, insisted his mother drop him at the end of the driveway. The rift continued to grow, reconciliation feeling less possible with each passing year.

In the aftermath, Gaylynn's half brother's bitterness grew sharper. When the shock of their father's death faded, his focus turned to what he felt entitled to: money. As the only son, he believed the responsibility of "carrying on the family name" gave him a greater claim than his sisters. In truth, he had always been upheld in their family dynamics as the treasured son, with three older sisters and a mother doting on him. Spoiled and almost always given what he wanted, he saw this as no different. He demanded the insurance payout, insisting it belonged to him. Their mother resisted at first, but he pressed hard, manipulating and wearing her down until she finally gave in. The sum was enough to support her comfortably for years, yet she handed it over. Watching it happen was like witnessing the same old pattern replayed: the loudest voice taking what it wanted while others yielded. For Gaylynn, it was another betrayal stacked on to so many before it, the kind of wound that doesn't bleed but still leaves its mark.

Weary of the unrest, Gaylynn knew she had to protect her own. She longed for distance, a clean break from the constant pull of family drama. When she and her husband found a house at the beach, it felt like the answer. The sound of waves rolling in at night replaced the noise of slammed doors. Salty breezes drifted through open windows, gulls cried overhead. For a while, it felt like escape.

She made the small house into a home. The scent of dinners lingered in the rooms, curtains billowed in the sea air, shells lined the windowsills. Though it was only a weekend place at first, she dreamed of the day they could make it their full-time home. For a brief season, the ocean washed some of the heaviness away. Yet the house was small, the walls soon felt tight, and the cost of maintaining two places made it clear they couldn't stretch the funds forever. Neighbors pressed too close, their presence a reminder that true respite still eluded her.

Her marriage carried the same strain it always had. They laughed, they fought, they circled the same weary patterns. Bills stacked high, tempers flared, responsibility pressed hard. The ocean softened some days, but it couldn't cure what lay beneath.

Still, Gaylynn refused bitterness. She decorated, she cooked, she celebrated. But restlessness stirred in her. She knew the beach house was only a stop along the way, not the refuge she longed for.

One evening, standing barefoot in the sand, she let the tide wash over her feet. The horizon stretched wide, the sun sinking into the water. She closed her eyes, breathing salt and wind, and felt the truth beneath the beauty: She was still searching for shelter, and no house—no matter how close to the ocean—could still the storms that lingered inside.

What she couldn't yet see was how each loss, each move, each attempt to build a refuge was preparing her. God was already at work, planting resilience in her spirit, even as she stood on the shoreline longing for peace.

CHAPTER 7

SEARCHING FOR PARADISE THROUGH THE STORM

"My peace I give you. I do not give to you as the world gives. Do not let your hearts be troubled and do not be afraid." — John 14:27

In time, Gaylynn and her husband decided to let the beach house go. It had given them weekends of escape and the hope of something more permanent, but given the strain of maintaining two households, the beach house was only ever a stop along the way.

Letting it go left Gaylynn longing for more than just a change of scenery. She wanted an open horizon in a deeper sense—room to breathe, space that wasn't hemmed in by neighbors' fences or crowded by the constant pull of family turmoil. A ranchette seemed to offer what she craved: space and tranquility.

At the height of their success, Gaylynn and her second husband finally touched the dream they had chased for so long: a ranchette in the country. To make it possible, they sold their primary home and poured everything into this new beginning. After years of hustling, patching things together, and scraping by, its purchase gave them a sense of accomplishment that felt almost foreign. The land stretched wide around them, quiet and steady. For once, they had space, and with it came the promise of peace, though only on the surface.

On the ranchette, that dream seemed, at last, to take a shape they could hold. The land stretched out wide and honest, fences drawing clean lines, the drive crunching beneath tires in a rhythm that sounded like arrival. Mornings came with fog lifting in thin bands from the low spots, coffee steaming from a chipped mug on the porch rail. By afternoon, eucalyptus woke up in the sun and sent its scent across the property in quiet waves. Evenings gathered in long washes of amber and violet. From the road, the place could pass for a postcard; up close, it was a lived-in triumph—maintenance lists taped near the phone, a drawer full of warranties and repair receipts, a fresh coil of hose under the spigot. Because tomorrow always asks for something: sometimes small, sometimes everything.

The property itself was beautiful, though it carried its share of responsibilities. Fences leaned and needed mending. Roof shingles gave way to the first heavy rain. The well pump rattled and groaned, reminding them it couldn't be taken for granted. But those challenges felt different from the ones that had come before—less like survival and more like the price of success. On good days, the air smelled faintly of walnut trees and tilled earth, the kind of scent that wrapped itself around the bones and breathed of steadiness. In the evenings, the sun sank into a wash of violet and gold, brushing the hills by an unseen hand.

Their finances still swung between feast and famine, but the feasts were bigger now, long stretches of prosperity where money flowed and the stress seemed lighter. Friends and family visited often, welcomed by Gaylynn's warmth and the openness of the land. She had a way of making the ranchette feel like the center of something, a place where people could gather, laugh, and stay until the porch light was the only lamp burning.

She and her husband had built something beautiful, and Gaylynn surrounded herself with laughter and created memories that would last a lifetime. The work they had poured into long hours and hard decisions finally began to show its return—steady income, a home they were proud of, even the breathing room to travel.

It was in that season that Belize entered the picture—not just as an idea, but as a second home. Buying a place there felt like proof that all their years of hustling had paid off. Sun, water that refused to remain only one shade of blue, air so warm it worked its way into your shoulders and loosened what life had bound tight—Belize became her sanctuary. Time there bent in Gaylynn's favor. The horizon drew a clean line extending forever. Everything tasted brighter: fruit cut in generous wedges, fish grilled so fresh the ocean still clung to it, rice and beans that made the table feel abundant without trying, and handmade corn tortillas still warm from the corner vendor. Music lived in the street, rising and wandering, laughing to itself in the dark.

Friends and family were drawn into the magic of Belize too, visiting whenever they could. Belize had a way of opening everyone up—laughter carrying on the warm air, long meals stretching into the night, a closeness ordinary life rarely allowed. One year, our family joined Gaylynn's for Christmas and New Year's, a trip that still stands in my memory as a string of sunlit days threaded with laughter, the air salted with sea and citrus. We lingered for ten unforgettable days, basking in the brightness of the island. Mornings began with coffee under wide skies, afternoons filled with boating and spearfishing, and evenings drifted into long meals that tasted of char, citrus, and salt.

Gaylynn's younger sister, brother-in-law, and several close friends were there as well. The aura was like a festival more than a vacation—an abundance of joy and togetherness, the kind of carefree happiness that had so often eluded Gaylynn in her early years. For those days, it seemed as though the island itself was intent on giving her what life had too often withheld: simplicity, safety, and wholeness.

The highlight of that trip came when Gaylynn arranged for an all-day catamaran cruise. It was meant to be an adults-only adventure, a chance for us to let go completely. We were excited, assuming we'd have the boat to ourselves. But when we boarded, we quickly realized another group had already claimed the prime spot at the front. The crew directed us toward the back, and for a moment it seemed we'd spend the day divided.

But that was never Gaylynn's way. She flashed that mischievous grin and said, "Oh, no, we're not splitting up. Watch this." Without hesitation, she strode to the front of the boat in her signature bikini, her laugh already softening the distance between strangers. Within minutes, she was chatting with the other group as if she'd known them for years. Her charm was effortless, her presence radiant. People leaned toward her instinctively, caught up in the current she created. Soon, everyone was laughing together, drinks in hand, the barrier between "us" and "them" dissolving.

Then, with her trademark boldness and grace, she asked, smiling, if the rest of us could join them at the front. They didn't just agree; they practically insisted, moving their gear with laughter as if it had been their idea all along. It was pure Gaylynn: fearless, captivating, and disarmingly kind, able to turn awkwardness into laughter and strangers into friends in a matter of minutes.

That afternoon, stretched out across the catamaran with sun warming our faces and waves glittering below, felt like wings. We traded stories, laughed until our cheeks hurt, and let the wind whip through our hair. Every moment was saturated with the kind of light-hearted ease that had always been rare in Gaylynn's life. For once, the world leaned toward joy instead of struggle. It wasn't just that one trip, either. Belize became a gathering place—a home they returned to often, filling its rooms with family and friends, the laughter spilling out into warm nights. For Gaylynn, those visits were more than vacations; they were reminders that life could hold both beauty and belonging. In time, the island would mean even more, becoming the refuge she turned to when everything else fell apart.

But on this trip, the meaning was simpler. Gaylynn was wholly herself: magnetic, playful, fearless in the most disarming way.

Wherever she went, a circle formed, not because she demanded it but because she made space for people to be at ease. That day, with the bow to ourselves and the island stepping toward us on the horizon, she looked like a woman who had wrung joy from the world simply by asking for it. We reached the other island in time for a lazy lunch, enjoying time with family, and getting to know new friends. As we were leaving, we held one last gaze that tried to capture the impossible blue of the water. On the long glide back, even the boat itself seemed reluctant to return us to shore.

If you saw only photographs from that trip, you would swear they were proof that life had finally become easy. But photographs lie by omission. They hold the brightness but not the shadow. We look suntouched and free. The glow leans toward us. It would be tempting to let those images tell the whole story. But even then, ease was only part of the truth. The beauty was real, and so was the other piece—the heaviness Gaylynn carried that didn't fit into pictures. It sat just beneath her laughter, invisible to almost everyone, but unmistakable if you knew what to watch for. It was a quietness around the eyes when music faded. It was the way her shoulders lifted for a second before she remembered to put them down. The island didn't erase any of that, but it gave her a place where heaviness could momentarily resolve.

For in the midst of such brightness, a quieter truth hovered beneath the surface. Gaylynn carried it with her always—the relentless heaviness of her past. The traumas of her childhood, the grief she had endured, the disappointments that had piled one upon another— none of it disappeared in the sun. She masked it well, laughing louder than most, telling stories with sparkle in her eyes. But those who knew her best could still sense it, like a shadow stretched thin beneath the brilliance of the day.

Belize was a reprieve, not an erasure. The ocean wrapped her in peace, but peace could only last so long before reality called her back. Even at the height of her success—surrounded by beauty, loved by friends, enjoying prosperity—she carried a restlessness. She knew deep down that no trip, no house, no island could undo the fractures of her past.

Still, those days mattered. They were gifts, moments of reprieve that reminded her she was more than what she had endured. Standing on the deck of that catamaran, wind lifting her hair, sun catching the sparkle of her smile, Gaylynn seemed untouchable: bold, striking, fearless. And in many ways, she was.

This was the crest of the wave for them. Work paid off in ways it never had before. Gaylynn and her family had dinners out where conversation was easy from start to finish. They spent evenings on the porch when the air-cooled ankles and coyotes stitched the distance with their thin songs and you could believe, for a stretch, that steadiness might truly be here to stay.

In hindsight, I can see those years as a mountaintop season for them—Gaylynn's mountaintop season. Gaylynn and her second husband moved through stretches of calm as well, shared projects that made them laugh like they used to, errands run with comfortable silence riding shotgun, the kind of small teamwork that made a house feel alive. Other days slipped back into the harder rhythm—words held too long, then held too tightly; a door closed more firmly than necessary; the quiet that arrives when neither person wants to spend more words than the moment is worth. Still, the good days were good, and there were many of them. She refused to let the heavy parts define the whole.

What I remember most from that season is how intentional she became with peace. She could not control the past and knew better than to pretend. She could not secure the future and had learned what it cost to try. But she could choose what music drifted from the next room. She could choose to repot her favorite plants when the budget said there were wiser choices, or acquire a new couch instead of caring for personal needs, because beauty argues with despair in a language despair can't answer. She could choose to stand at the fence line during the sunrise and let God's quiet find her. The apostle John's words—*My peace I give you . . . not as the world gives*—felt less like a verse on a page and more like the daily practice of opening her hands.

Belize made its way back to the ranchette. It visited in small ways: A bright cloth on the table. A photo that insisted there was a place where water wore the color of new joy. The memory of that catamaran afternoon—how a door opened because she asked, how people moved because she made the moving feel like a gift. Those things mattered. They were not pretend. They were mercy.

From the outside, anyone might have said she'd made it—land to tend, a home that welcomed, friends gathered close, a stretch of prosperity, an island home they returned to often, a place that felt like proof. And yes, it was a kind of making it. But the heart knows what photographs cannot say. Ground looks solid until the weather changes; then you learn which parts were bedrock and which were simply hardpacked earth. If there was a tremor ahead, we couldn't hear it yet. The horizon looked ordinary. The fence lines held. The lists were reasonable. No one watching her lean against that porch rail, elbow set, eyes on the rising sun, would have guessed what was moving toward her.

CHAPTER 8

BREAKING POINT

*"When all that surrounds you is broken, it's hard
not to believe you've reached the end."*

Success is a fickle thing. For years, Gaylynn and her second husband had worked and dreamed together, closing real estate deals, hosting parties for their friends and family, and taking their daughters on trips that felt like proof they had made it. At home, they were a strong parenting team—tag-teaming homework, showing up at school events, going to horse shows, and cheering from the bleachers at games. From the outside, the life they built looked solid, even enviable. However, as the market shifted and financial pressures mounted, the fault lines in their marriage widened. Her property management and real estate businesses, once steady, staggered under the market's decline, pulling their marriage with them. What had once been a shared vision of prosperity and partnership slowly hardened into a battleground of blame, frustration, and distance. The tension between them—always simmering just beneath the surface—rose toward its breaking point.

During one of those tense stretches, Gaylynn took her girls to their home in Belize for a short vacation. The island had always been her refuge, a place where the salt air seemed to untangle what life had knotted. One afternoon she climbed onto a Jet Ski, deciding to race against the boat her daughters were riding in. True to who she is, Gaylynn was always up for an adventure, ready to turn an ordinary afternoon into something unforgettable. If it made her heart pound faster, all the better; and this was no exception. Laughter and spray filled the air until, in an instant, the fun turned dangerous. She struck a sandbar at full speed, the crack of the impact undeniable, throwing her violently into the water. Semiconscious, the salt water burning her throat, she floated until the boat captain spotted her and pulled her to safety.

Though dazed and injured, Gaylynn waved away concern in her characteristic fashion. She insisted she was fine, brushing off pain that would have surely leveled someone else. She tried to continue the trip, but the discomfort grew unbearable, forcing her to cut it short. Back home, she carried on with the same determination, hiding her pain behind busyness and insisting she didn't need medical help. Yet the pain refused to be ignored.

A few weeks later, her husband took the girls out of town to a sporting event, leaving Gaylynn home alone. By then her condition had worsened to the point she could barely walk. She dragged her leg behind her, feeling almost nothing below her hip. Waves of nausea doubled her over, and she vomited again and again. Her husband had dismissed her pain as sciatica, telling her it would pass, but deep inside she knew something was terribly wrong.

Desperate, she called her younger sister. True to her blunt, teasing nature, her sister answered with a half joke meant to cut through the fear: "Okay, Quasimodo, are you finally ready to go to the doctor?" Reluctantly, Gaylynn agreed.

When the MRI results came back, everything shifted. She was rushed into emergency back surgery. The surgeon fused her spine with a steel rod, stabilizing an injury that should have left her unable to walk. She remained in the hospital for four days, stunned by the severity of what she had narrowly escaped. The doctor told her plainly: Had she waited much longer, she would have been paralyzed. Even with the surgery, she would live with permanent "foot drop." The surgeon shook his head, half in disbelief, and joked that she should buy a lottery ticket; she was the luckiest patient he had ever met.

Once again, Gaylynn had defied the odds. Two years later, she trained for and completed a full marathon. She proved to herself and everyone else that she could outrun pain, but not the shadows gathering inside. As her body mended, her marriage came undone. The healing on the outside couldn't mask the fractures that had been growing within.

Her marriage—already strained by years of infidelity on both sides, the presence of drugs and alcohol, and the relentless weight of financial pressure—could not withstand the fracture. The tension that had lingered for so long finally broke. Their separation became final, leaving Gaylynn once again to face life on her own.

The unraveling did not stop there. Depression crept in, heavy and suffocating. Everything she had fought to hold together seemed to be slipping through her fingers. Instead of reaching for the God she had known had been with her since childhood, she turned inward and downward, leaning harder on the painkillers prescribed after her back surgery. What had begun as relief from physical pain quickly became a way to quiet the emotional ache. She numbed herself with whatever she could find, tumbling deeper into addiction.

The consequences spread outward like ripples from a stone dropped in still water. Her relationships strained, even with her daughters. It's hard to imagine they could have understood what was happening to their mother, why the woman who had once carried them with such strength was unraveling before their eyes. Gaylynn—ashamed, exhausted, and unable to explain—grew more erratic. Friends and family reached for her, but she pushed them away.

I tried to bridge the gap myself. I arranged for her to see a Christian therapist, even paying for the appointment. She agreed, attended once, but never returned. "Counseling just isn't for me," she told me. Whether it was fear, denial, or simply the weight of facing so much trauma at once, she could not bring herself to sit in that space of honesty.

But what she was facing was not only emotional; it was spiritual.

One night, alone in her bed, Gaylynn woke to a terror she still struggles to describe. She felt hands around her throat, pressing the air from her lungs. No one else was in the house, yet she was certain she was being choked. Panic surged, but she couldn't scream. Later, she would call it a demonic attack. Maybe it was the by-product of trauma and medication. Perhaps depression gave it form. Or possibly it was what it felt like to wrestle with evil itself. Whatever it was, the fear was real, and it left a scar on her spirit she carried for years.

Eventually, the burden of relentless strain grew unbearable. At her lowest, Gaylynn attempted to take her own life.

She swallowed a dangerous number of pills and climbed behind the wheel, driving with one desperate purpose: to drown herself in a lake. Her younger sister and I were both on the phone with her as she drove. We begged her to tell us where she was. She refused. Her voice was distant, resigned. Through tears she repeated, "Leave me alone."

But we couldn't.

Her sister frantically called the highway patrol, desperate to track her location. I kept dialing, refusing to let the line go quiet. Each time she answered, even incoherently, I held on, knowing the connection might be the only thread between life and death. My prayers became breaths: *Lord, keep her alive. Don't let this be the end.*

By the grace of God, officers found her in time. She was parked in a rest stop at the entrance to a lake. Trucks hissed by on the highway and gravel crunched under her shoes as she stepped out with determination to carry out her plan: She was going to drive into the water and let the heaviness of the car take her under. But before she did, she decided to walk around the parking area. I know without hesitation that we all experienced divine intervention . . . once again. The highway patrol got to her as she was returning to her car and rushed her to the hospital. There she was, placed under suicide watch, given—for the first time—a forced pause. A place to confront, even briefly, the pain she had carried too long.

When I visited, she was already waiting, peering at me through the narrow window of her hospital door. Tears streamed down her cheeks as she murmured, "I knew you'd come." We sat together, and she began to open up, with trepidation, about the burden she bore. I listened, prayed, and tried to help her see a way forward. But the wall around her heart was still too high. She wasn't ready. Healing would have to wait. Even so, I knew in my heart and clung to my faith that God wasn't done with her story.

When she left the hospital, life no longer resembled what it once had; the losses and fractures had reshaped everything around her. It was then she began to consider what had always pulled at her: the island. Gaylynn made the decision that would mark a new chapter. Her daughters were young adults, beginning their own lives. She chose to leave the US and move full-time to Belize. She was searching for a new way forward, and Belize seemed to offer it.

For her, Belize was more than a getaway. It was a place to breathe again, to put distance between herself and the ghosts of what she had endured. To her daughters, though, it must have been confusing and painful—watching their mother leave at a time when they needed her close, especially in the midst of a messy divorce. Gaylynn believed she was choosing survival, independence, and a chance to redefine herself. But to her girls, it likely felt like abandonment; I know I would have felt that way at their age. Just as quickly as success had built a life that looked secure, it splintered, leaving only choices that carried their own kind of loss.

Her younger sister was furious. We spoke often about it. I reminded her that Gaylynn was strong-willed, that she needed room to heal, and that she was an adult free to make her own decisions. But my words didn't ease the sting. For her sister, Gaylynn's move was deepening the fracture in a bond already strained.

"Americans who live in Belize are always running from something," her younger sister once said. And run Gaylynn did. She ran from pain, from betrayal, from her own reflection in the mirror. The island represented both reprieve and escape. It was a place where she could shed the remnants of the life she had built—and lost—and start over, even if the starting over meant leaving wounds behind that would take years to face.

CHAPTER 9

RUNNING AND RETURNING

"You may encounter many defeats, but you must not be defeated." — Maya Angelou

Gaylynn's move to Belize had started as an escape—a way to put distance between herself and the ruins of a marriage, the sting of betrayal, and the ghosts of all she had endured. At first, island life seemed to offer everything she longed for: sunlit days, water clear enough to blur the line between sky and sea.

Mornings began slow—coffee on a small balcony, the air already warm, the sea laying down its steady hush. Vendors rolled ice chests past her door, calling out prices for fruit, and a radio somewhere down the street drifted through two songs at once. She learned the shortcuts through the alleys, the quiet hours at the market, the way the breeze changed direction at dusk. She had returned often with her family, and each visit reminded her how the island asked very little beyond showing up. That felt like mercy.

But paradise has shadows too.

The island welcomed her with open arms, and in those early months she threw herself into its rhythm. Yet beneath the beauty, her old demons followed. Alcohol flowed freely, and drugs were as accessible as the waves on the shore. In that environment, it was easy to forget the promises she had once made to herself.

Her relationships reflected the instability within. She became involved with a man whose charm masked a darker truth: He was deeply entangled in drugs. He knew everyone and was known by everyone, the kind of man who waved before you even recognized him. Nights with him came bright and easy at first: a table outside, music threading through conversation, promises tossed out like spare limes. But the fun had a seam. She felt it even while laughing—how the room tilted when the bottle remained too long, how the plans kept sliding to "later." It was the same old bargain in a prettier place, and she took it because for a while it worked and she felt safe with him.

What began as romance slipped into destruction. Parties stretched late into the night, her laughter loud but hollow, her glass never empty. Some evenings she promised herself just one. One became two, then the edge blurred and with it her intentions. She hated waking to a room she barely recognized—the sour after-smell of spilled alcohol, the fan ticking, the light too white. She wrote lists mentally, would review them over and over in her mind, and still couldn't make a plan hold.

When that relationship ended, she pivoted hard toward sobriety and held it—steadily—for a few years. But the island kept offering new beginnings, and eventually she met a local islander.

At first, he seemed charming and attentive, offering companionship in a place where she had no family to lean on. But beneath the surface, danger lingered—danger she didn't initially see. Many of her island friends warned her, saying he wasn't a good man, but Gaylynn brushed off their concerns, dismissing them as judgmental or jealous. She had always seen the good in people, often to a fault. Even as a child, she gravitated toward those who were different, misunderstood, or cast aside. She welcomed misfits, dreamers, and wounded souls into her heart and home without hesitation. It was both her gift and her curse.

Soon, the pattern reappeared. She was partying again—drugs and alcohol blurring the days. No matter how much I wanted to pull her home, I knew she wouldn't listen. Gaylynn has always been determined—some would say hardheaded. We used to joke that God would have to drop a brick house on her head before she'd finally hear the message. The truth was harder: She had to deal with her demons herself, in her own time, even if that meant walking straight through the danger she already sensed.

It started with this man correcting her in small ways—how she should speak, where she should sit, who she should greet. Then came the sharper moments, the kind that made her go still. She learned the patterns of his moods, how to read the set of his jaw, when to disappear into another room and count the seconds. The ocean kept doing what it does—coming and going as if nothing had changed—while inside the walls she tried to make herself unnoticeable, harder to hit with words or with hands. His affection hardened into control, and control into violence.

While she was in Belize, I prayed constantly. Sometimes it was a full prayer; sometimes it was only her name spoken softly while I folded laundry or sat at a red light. I asked God to put people in her path who would tell her the truth gently and keep her safe when she would not keep herself from harm's way.

The cycle was merciless. Nights that began with laughter ended with bruises and apologies. She told herself she could handle it, that she had endured worse and survived. But every blow—whether from fist or word—chipped away at her spirit. Friends urged her to leave, prayed she would find her way out. She smiled, deflected, and remained.

Once, when the fear finally outweighed the excuses, she ran. With no money of her own—he controlled everything—she leaned on the kindness of a friend to help her get from Belize to Mexico, and then on toward the United States. But the quest took a dark turn. In Mexico, she climbed into a taxi, hoping distance would save her. It didn't. The driver assaulted her before she could reach the border, tormenting her with a knife, forcing her to stay the night with him, demanding she say she loved him. Terrified for her life, she complied. Her escape unraveled almost as soon as it began.

The next day he finally drove her to the border. Shaken and violated, she crossed and caught a bus home. Her mother met her at the bus station and took her to a clinic, where the paper on the exam table crackled beneath her, cold against her skin as she endured the indignities of a rape kit and screening. For a few days she remained close, cocooned in safety. But shame convinced her she was too broken, too unworthy. Within the week, she returned to the very place she had fought to escape: back to Belize, and back to him.

Then came the night that nearly ended her—not by her own hand, but his. She called me, her voice faint and uneven, whispering, so I knew she was in danger. The beating had been horrific, leaving her body battered and her spirit crushed. She told me she could quietly make her way to the airport, but once again, she had no money. Without hesitation, I arranged a flight. Hours later she was back on US soil—battered, exhausted, but alive.

She stayed with me for a few weeks, then with friends. For the first time in a long while, she felt safe—surrounded by family, by love, by me. But she never fully severed the tie. She kept in contact with him, convinced he would change. And then, without telling anyone, she disappeared. I found out only when my daughter called to say she'd seen a post on social media: Gaylynn was back in Belize. I hadn't known. Within a few short weeks, she was there again—back to him.

Her younger sister's anger boiled over. To her, Gaylynn's choices seemed like betrayal stacked on betrayal, in many ways mirroring what had fractured the bond between Gaylynn and her half sister. Different circumstances, same ache: choices born of survival, but walls built of pain and unhealed wounds. Only later did I realize how those fractures echoed each other. With both her half sister and her younger sister, the break came not from lack of love but from choices too heavy to carry, decisions that grew into barriers neither side could easily climb. It was as if the survival instincts that once bonded Gaylynn and her younger sister eventually became the very factor that pushed them apart. The pattern was painful to witness—how the wounds of one generation seemed to ripple forward, creating fresh divides.

Even as she tried to piece her life back together, the grip of addiction was not easily broken. She hid pills in obvious places just to prove she wasn't hiding them. She told herself she could quit on Tuesday, then pushed Tuesday further down the calendar. Shame made everything louder. Painkillers lingered in her system, alcohol beckoned, and memories of abuse clung like damp clothes that refused to dry.

What gave her strength in those years was not the perfection of her circumstances but her refusal to stop trying. Every setback pressed her lower, but each time she found a way to rise—sometimes staggering, sometimes crawling, but never surrendering completely. Each bruise, each apology, each morning after only deepened the question: What would it take to be free?

Faith was often faint, a quiet muttering more than a shout. Sometimes all she managed was a sentence—*Help me*—mouthed into a dark room. Other times she opened the Bible my daughter bought for her—not to read, but to let it rest open on her lap like a light she didn't yet know how to switch on. She could not explain why God's nearness rose strongest when she felt least deserving, only that it did, like a tide.

Eventually, she knew she couldn't keep going as she was. The pull of the island, the cycle of violence, the grip of addiction; it was killing her by degrees. With nothing left to lose, she left Belize once more, this time to stay with her biological father.

Despite his past, including years in prison for drug distribution near an elementary school—she sought his support, perhaps hoping for connection or redemption in a place she'd never had the chance to explore. Staying with him for a few months gave her space to breathe. Away from the upheaval, she could finally step back and see her life with clarity.

With a respite away from the dark undercurrent of the island, she was able to stop using drugs and alcohol, leaning on what she called a "higher power." Without destructive influences circling her, the fog began to lift. For the first time in years, she could imagine living differently.

While Gaylynn was away, she allowed two young women to stay in her home in Belize but warned them about her abusive ex. Despite her warnings, one of them was targeted by him and became his next victim.

Gaylynn had first met the young woman on the last day of a yoga retreat. The young woman arrived with no money or food. True to her nature, Gaylynn gave her everything she had left, then helped contact the young lady's father to purchase a ticket home. In return, the young woman promised to paint a mural on Gaylynn's fence in Belize. She kept her word to Gaylynn and returned to Belize— unaware of the danger waiting.

Not long after, Gaylynn's ex assaulted the young woman, leaving her shaken and afraid. News of it reached Gaylynn quickly. When Gaylynn learned about the assault, she prayed for provision to return and face the situation head-on. God answered through the kindness of another woman, who made her way back to the island possible. This time, Gaylynn was not the victim. She stood beside the young woman, urging her to press charges and making sure her ex would finally be held accountable.

For so long, she had struggled to save herself. In helping another woman escape, she discovered a strength she hadn't fully embraced. Something old stirred in her—the same instinct that once made her shield her younger sister. Only now it wasn't just for family; it was for any woman caught in cycles of fear and pain.

Even in her darkest moments, she knew deep down that God had not left her. He had guided from afar, waiting for her to turn back. Yet she struggled to believe in the Father's unconditional love. Years of abuse at the hands of men had hardened her against that thought.

Still, from that point forward, everything began to change. She left substances behind and committed herself to emotional and spiritual restoration. She pursued yoga, completing her certification, finding in the practice a tool for strength and peace. More than anything, she found purpose: helping other women find their own strength.

This was the beginning of her true transformation—her pilgrimage from survivor to healer. But her quest was not over. The greatest battles of her life still lay ahead.

CHAPTER 10

IN THE SHADOW OF THE PAST

"There is no pit so deep, that God's love is not deeper still." — Corrie ten Boom

When Gaylynn first ran to Belize after her second divorce, her daughters were already young adults, but that didn't mean they no longer needed their mother. Her departure carved an ache that shaped them in ways she would never fully know. Hurt, anger, and bitterness followed her, and with them the permanent fracturing of her deep bond with her younger sister. To Gaylynn, going to Belize felt like the only choice left to preserve her sanity. To those she left behind, it looked like abandonment. She thought about the ordinary things she would miss: birthdays, Sunday calls, the moments when her girls might have needed her voice most. Silence on the other end of the line was harder than shouting. Now there was only absence, a silence so sharp it felt like rejection, though she knew she had been the one to leave. With her younger sister, the connection had once been steadfast: late-night talks shared under blankets, promises made in the dark that they would always look out for each other, and secrets they swore an oath to always keep hidden. To lose that closeness was like losing a part of herself she didn't know how to replace.

She had been drowning in the wreckage of her marriage, the failure of her businesses, and the embarrassment of a life crumbling in full view of others. Running to Belize was less about a dream of island life and more about survival. She wasn't ready—maybe not even able—to face the trauma that had been buried since childhood. So, she left, choosing distance over confrontation.

Yet leaving her family behind wasn't only a physical act; it was an emotional break. Even in moments of relief, guilt was a weight she could not shake. For years she wondered whether her daughters believed she had abandoned them, whether the choice she had made would ever be worth the pain it had caused. As much as she longed for grace, the questions never let her rest.

When she returned to Belize for the second time, she accepted that this time she was there to stay. The guilt of the past still clung to her, but she had crossed a threshold in her spirit. There was no going back to the life she had.

On the island she pieced together a livelihood. She worked in a dive shop, her skin salted by the air and her hair sunlit by days spent near the water. She began teaching yoga, her body moving into postures that steadied her mind as much as her muscles. Yoga was the opposite of the dive shop—quiet mornings on a shaded deck, the sea a steady percussion in the background. Her voice, calm and steady, surprised even her. In the dive shop, tanks clanged against each other, the floor always slick with saltwater, visitors dropping in with wide-eyed excitement. Travelers bustled in and out, their excitement spilling into the humid air, chattering about reefs and sea turtles. Gaylynn smiled, ringing up masks and snorkels, pretending she belonged in the rush of it all. But it was in the yoga studio, an open-air deck shaded by palms, where she felt serenity. Students spread their mats while the ocean kept time in the background. She guided them through each posture, her voice steady in ways her spirit hadn't always been. At the end of class, when she asked them to close their eyes and breathe, she often lingered in the silence herself, surprised to find fragments of peace taking root.

From the outside, it seemed like Gaylynn was living a postcard life on a tropical island: palm trees swaying against wide skies, stretches of crystal-clear blue water, and sunsets pouring gold into the sea. But, Gaylynn often reminded those who envied her life, there was an underbelly to Belize that most people didn't see or understand.

Temptations were everywhere—drugs, alcohol, unhealthy relationships—and it took daily resolve not to slide back into old patterns. She learned to walk past, muttering her refusals more to herself than to anyone else. Some nights the temptation pressed close. Laughter floated out of the beachside bars, the smell of rum sharp in the air, old friends waving her over with easy grins. "Just one," they'd say, and the memory of what "just one" had cost her rose like a tide. She would shake her head, eyes forward, breathing a prayer under her breath as she kept walking. Each refusal felt small, but strung together they became a lifeline.

Sobriety for her wasn't a single decision but a series of them. Each morning brought its own battle. She knew what it was to wake up to regret, to let shame drive her choices, and she refused to live there anymore. This time she surrounded herself with people who supported her new path, who reminded her of her promises to herself and to God. She refused to let the turmoil of her past dictate her future. Still, the struggle was constant. Some days memories of her past threatened to swallow her, and the pull of old escapes tightened around her. But she chose again and again to move forward.

Helping others became her mission. Gaylynn often said, "I have shelter over my head and beans to eat. I have more than most." By that she meant even in her leanest moments she had more than enough, and it freed her to give. Sometimes it was nothing more than making beans stretch far enough to feed two households instead of one. Other times it meant sitting on a porch late into the night, letting another woman cry without interruption. She gave out of what little she had, but she gave as if it were abundance. Helping others did not erase her own wounds, but in giving comfort she found her own heart softening. Each story of survival she heard became another reminder that she was not alone, that healing could grow even in the harshest soil. She reached out to women who had fallen into the same traps she once had, offering them a lifeline. She listened when they felt unheard, and when pain silenced them, she held space for them right where they were. And in the act of helping, she found herself growing stronger.

Her commitment to the young woman attacked by her ex-boy-friend became the fuel that kept her going. Navigating the legal system to make sure he was arrested and remained incarcerated gave her purpose. This time, her life on the island was different. She was sober, clear-eyed, and determined. She was no longer living in reaction to her pain but in defiance of it.

This clarity also extended to her family. Gaylynn began making intentional efforts to mend the broken fences she had left behind. She remained in close contact with her middle daughter, who had long been the bridge between Gaylynn and the rest of the family. Their conversations were frequent, sometimes several times a week, filled with both the ordinary and the heartfelt. The calls ranged from the everyday—recipes, recent boyfriends, the weather—to the tender: words that let her know she was still loved. Gaylynn clung to each conversation, replaying them after the line went quiet, as if listening again could make up for the years she had lost. Sometimes she would replay the snippets of what her daughter said—stories about work, a joke, even a turn of phrase—just to hold them in her heart. In lonely evenings, she would recall her daughter's words, hearing her daughter's voice in her mind, clinging to the connection as if the words themselves carried warmth. It was a fragile bridge, but it was enough to remind her that love still reached across the miles. Through her middle daughter she remained connected to her other two, though the distance between them still ached.

Those calls reminded her she was not alone, even as the larger work of rebuilding continued. Gaylynn treasured that connection. It did not erase the ache of past choices, but it was a thread of grace she held on to tightly. She hoped one day the wounds between her and her girls would soften enough to let love in again. Until then, she kept choosing the small steps: making the call, writing the text message, staying present however she could.

Each step she took on this new path was a step away from the turmoil that had once defined her life. Sobriety was not only abstaining from substances but living with intention—refusing to return to the destruction that had nearly claimed her. Rebuilding wasn't about replacing what had been lost; it was about creating something new from the pieces still in her hands.

Belize gave her space, but it also demanded resilience. The beauty of the island stood beside its harshness. In that tension, Gaylynn began to see herself more clearly. She was strong, resilient, and filled with grace—not because she had avoided suffering, but because she had walked through it and was still standing.

She was learning that brokenness does not disqualify us; it becomes the soil where redemption can take root. Helping others reminded her of that truth. Every woman she encouraged, every small victory she celebrated with them, reflected back to her the possibility of her own healing.

This was the heart of her story: not perfection, not an unbroken story, but a relentless pursuit of purpose in the shadow of her past. She was no longer only surviving. She was rebuilding.

Storms came quickly on the island, the sky blackening without warning, palm trees bending low. Yet within an hour the sun might return, drenching everything in light again. Her life felt much the same—beauty and harshness pressed side by side. She knew better than to mistake calm skies for permanence. Somewhere beyond the horizon, storms were gathering. She remembered once watching a storm roll across the island, clouds black and heavy, rain slamming against the roof until her own voice disappeared beneath the noise. She waited it out, the air thick with the scent of salt and earth. An hour later the sun returned, so bright it seemed impossible the storm had ever come. Gaylynn stood in the doorway, wet ground steaming around her, and thought about how life could feel exactly the same— destruction one moment, radiance the next.

CHAPTER 11

TIGHT HUGS AND MOMENTS TO CHERISH

"Enjoy the little things in life, for one day you may look back and realize they were the big things." — Robert Brault

Life had begun to settle for Gaylynn in Belize. The young woman who had been attacked by Gaylynn's ex-boyfriend had returned home after the legal case was resolved, and with her departure came a quieter rhythm, leaving Gaylynn alone on the island for the first time in years. Temptations still lingered at the edges, but she had carved out a life that felt steadier than the tumultuous one she had once known.

During this season, her middle daughter began urging her to come home for a visit. Their conversations often ended with the same plea: "Mom, you need to come back, just for a little while." At first, Gaylynn brushed her off. She had excuses ready: work, commitments, no money. But her daughter's persistence never waned. Each time they spoke, the invitation was there again, like a door left open.

One afternoon, standing at the sink with her hands in warm, soapy water, Gaylynn heard it, a voice so clear it startled her: *Go. Go home and see your daughter.* She knew it was God's voice—undeniable. The moment left no room for doubt. She dried her hands, picked up the phone, and called her daughter. "I'll come," she said. "I'll be there in August."

She had only two hundred dollars to her name, but she packed a backpack, boarded a flight, and left the island. She didn't know why the timing mattered so much, but she trusted that God did.

When she stepped off the plane, I was waiting. Our eyes met, and her tears came immediately. The smell of coffee and exhaust clung to the humid air as travelers bustled around us, dragging luggage and calling out greetings. For a moment the noise fell away, leaving only the two of us in that crowded terminal. On the drive home, the silence stretched as wide as the highway. I gripped the steering wheel, glancing sideways at her, wondering if this visit would end like the others—with hope quickly unraveling. Years of hurt and mistrust sat between us like a wall we had both grown too weary to climb. Choices she had made, things left unsaid, and the distance time creates when hearts stay guarded. Still, I had heard God's own voice in my heart reminding me: *Love her, or leave her.* So, I loved her.

She had already arranged to stay with a friend, unsure whether I would welcome her back into my home. I drove her there, our conversation careful but lingering on the surface. I was not sure if I'd see her again while she was home, given everything that had happened between us. The years of hurt, the broken trust, the decisions that had left both of us scarred; it all lingered between us as an invisible wall, one we couldn't bring ourselves to breach.

After a few days of her being home, she asked to come over "to talk." I wasn't sure if she wanted to reconcile or if this was just a brief visit before she slipped back into her old life. A part of me feared the visit would end as it always had, with her returning to the upheaval of the island, leaving the pieces of our fractured relationship behind once again. We talked around the jagged edges of the past, circling back again and again to God's plan for her life. She admitted, with unflinching honesty, that she often questioned whether God was real at all. "If He is," she asked me, "why has He always felt so far away? Why does it seem like He abandoned me?"

Her questions were valid, born out of a life filled with turmoil, loss, and pain. I told her what I believed with all my heart—that God was real, that He loved her more than she could imagine, and that the seeming absence was never abandonment. Sometimes, I said, He waits for us to stop running.

Our conversation lingered long into the day and evening. She asked about salvation, about what it truly meant to be a Christian, about whether grace could really cover all that she had done. Finally, I asked the question that had been sitting on my heart: "Gaylynn, have you ever given your life to the Lord?"

She shook her head.

"Do you want to?"

There was no hesitation this time. She softly said, "Yes." Her voice cracked on that single word, a mixture of fear and longing. As we bowed our heads together, I could hear the faint whir of the refrigerator in the kitchen and the rustle of wind against the window-pane. It struck me how ordinary the moment looked: two close-knit cousins sitting side by side in a modest living room. Yet I knew heaven itself leaned close. My heart pounded as I prayed, the words halting but filled with urgency, and when she repeated them, her voice shook. For years I had carried her name to God in prayer, and now, at last, I heard her call on Him for herself.

Right there, in my living room, Gaylynn surrendered her life to Christ for the first time. Our words were simple but sincere. Tears streamed down her cheeks as we finished, and I pulled her into a hug that felt like both a beginning and a homecoming. A few years later, she affirmed that moment through baptism in our church.

She stayed a few more days in town, visiting friends and reconnecting with familiar places. Social media kept her tethered to a wide circle, and she shared her travels as a way of staying grounded in community. One of her closest friends, who often helped arrange her flights, asked her to stop in Texas on her way back to Belize to babysit her son for a few days. Gaylynn agreed; it was her nature to say yes.

But her real focus this trip was clear: time with her family, with her mother, and especially with her middle daughter.

Her visit with her mother was perhaps the most surprising. Their history was long and complicated, marked by tension, misunderstandings, and painful memories. Gaylynn had braced herself for another battle, another round of accusations or old wounds flaring up. Instead, something gentler unfolded. There was laughter, small and tentative at first, but real. Gaylynn later told me how her stomach was in knots as she walked up the uneven path to her mother's back door, rehearsing how she would hold her tongue if grievances surfaced. But when the door opened, her mother simply stepped back and gestured her in. They sat at the small kitchen table, coffee mugs between them. The conversation moved slowly at first, each word careful, but then memories crept in—fond ones. For the first time in years, the room felt lighter. For once, they sat together without knives drawn from memory. It wasn't complete healing, but it was something.

Afterward, she traveled several hours to see her daughter. This was the heart of the trip, the reason God had told her to come. Those days together were simple but radiant. They walked along the beach with sand warm beneath their feet, traded stories from childhood to the present, and laughed like no time had passed at all.

The beach was their shared sanctuary. Gaylynn loved watching her daughter run along the shore, hair flying in the wind, laughter ringing out above the roar of the waves. She still had the same youthful energy, still performed her signature one-handed cartwheels in the sand. Gaylynn clapped and laughed, the sight of her daughter's joy etching itself onto her heart. The gulls wheeled overhead, their cries sharp against the steady crash of waves. Sand clung to their skin, salt in the air mixed with sunscreen, and the ocean breeze carried the smell of possibility. Beaches had been sacred places for Gaylynn since childhood—where she had gone to escape, to think, to breathe. To share that space with her daughter felt like handing over a piece of herself, a reminder that joy could still be inherited even after years of heartache. "It wasn't just the beach or the laughter," Gaylynn would later reflect. "It was the bond. Those are the moments I'll always hold close to my heart."

They shared countless hugs in those short few days together—quick squeezes, lingering embraces, and everything in between. Each one felt like a balm, a physical reminder that love had not been erased by distance or time or life choices.

One afternoon, as their time together drew short, her daughter wrapped her arms tightly around Gaylynn's neck and held on. "I like to do this," she explained. "I tell my friends I have to hug my mom so tight because I never know when or if I'll see her again."

The words pierced Gaylynn's heart. She held her daughter longer, as though she could stop time with the strength of her embrace. Gaylynn breathed in the scent of her daughter's hair, salty from the beach and sweet with sunscreen, trying to memorize it. Her daughter's words etched themselves into her mind, indelible. It was more than a goodbye; it was a plea wrapped in love. Gaylynn pressed her face into her daughter's shoulder, willing the moment to last, knowing it couldn't. Some embraces carry the gravity of prophecy, even when you don't yet see the future they point to.

That was on the Friday of Labor Day weekend. Her daughter was excited, bringing summer to a close and looking forward to spending the long weekend at a well-known lake just across the state line with family and friends. It was shaping up to be a weekend of fun, connection, and all the good things in life. They had a plan, a future, and all the good things in life, the kind that seem endless until they aren't.

When the visit finally ended, Gaylynn carried with her the contentment of reconnection—of conversations that mattered, of laughter that healed, of hugs that lingered. She left for her next stop with a heart both heavy and full, cherishing every moment they had shared.

Gaylynn could not have known then how significant those days would become. She only knew they had been a gift. Love, once fractured, had been tenderly stitched together, thread by thread.

She looked forward with hope, unaware that life was about to change forever. The memory of those tight hugs and cherished moments would remain with her always, a lifeline she could cling to when grief came again.

She carried those embraces with her as she boarded her next flight, the sound of laughter still echoing in her ears. She couldn't have known the urgency of God's prompting, or why her daughter's hug had felt so gripping. But in time, we would all understand. For now, the memory of those days was enough—a tender mercy stitched into her story, holding her steady for what was coming.

She didn't know then that those hugs would become the last, or that the laughter they shared would echo against the silence of what was to come.

ACT III

WHEN THE UNTHINKABLE COMES

"Grief never asks permission before it breaks your life apart." — Anonymous

"THEY CAN'T FIND HER... THEY CAN'T FIND HER!"

The words tore through the phone line, carried by Gaylynn's screams, collapsing the air around me. Her voice was raw, frantic, unrelenting. It wasn't just sound; it was the sound of her world breaking open.

Some moments split a life in two: before and after. This was one of them. In an instant, the ground beneath her gave way, and nothing would ever return to what it had been.

Grief does not wait its turn. It does not knock politely. It crashes in unannounced, overturning every steady thing, rewriting every page that follows. I had thought the depths of her story were already profound, but I hadn't known the bottom could fall out this far.

The sound of Gaylynn's wail still lingers in my soul. It was the sound of a mother's heart tearing apart, a sound that could not be stilled, not even by distance. What followed was a season of loss and struggle so severe it would wound her life in ways I could never have imagined.

CHAPTER 12

IN THE BLINK OF AN EYE

"Every family has a day that changes everything. This was hers." — Unknown

On her flight to Texas, Gaylynn did something she rarely allowed herself—a momentary break from the constant noise of the world. She pressed the power button on her phone, silencing the pings and vibrations that tethered her to everything outside herself. For once, she gave herself permission to retreat.

The thrum of the airplane filled her ears, steady and low, like a backdrop of reassurance. The dimmed cabin lights cast long shadows over faces softened by sleep. She leaned back against the seat, the worn fabric cradling her body, put her sleep mask on, and tried to rest. It wasn't comfort exactly, but it was enough. For a few suspended hours, she allowed herself to breathe without demand, without interruption, without expectation. It felt almost luxurious, this pocket of stillness in the blur of airports, strained conversations, and the ache of missing home.

When the wheels touched down and the cabin filled with the metallic click of seat belts unfastening, her heart grew restless again. By the time she reached her friend's home late that night, fatigue pressed heavily on her limbs. The house was familiar and kind, filled with comforting scents that usually invited her to settle in. But even here, rest felt elusive. She and her friend traded a few words, their voices wrapped in the polite cadence of exhaustion: forced smiles, weary laughter, nothing that reached the depths of what either woman carried. When Gaylynn finally slipped between the sheets, her body gave in, but her mind wandered restless, circling questions she couldn't name. She longed for sleep to claim her fully, to grant her a reprieve.

The reprieve lasted only until morning.

When she finally pressed the button to turn her phone back on, the quiet world shattered. The screen lit up with missed calls, one after another—urgent, insistent, impossible to ignore. Notifications stacked like a wall she couldn't scale. Messages flooded in so quickly, the phone itself seemed to vibrate with fear. Her chest tightened as she scrolled, though she hadn't yet read enough to understand. She only knew, deep down, that something was terribly wrong.

Her friend, already aware of what had happened, moved swiftly. She gathered Gaylynn's essentials and booked the soonest flight, her movements efficient in the way of someone who knew there was no time to waste. The air in the house thickened with urgency, a silence undercut by the rustle of bags being zipped and the frantic tapping of a keyboard.

That same Sunday morning of Labor Day weekend, I was at home in California, slipping on my shoes, preparing to head to church with my husband. The sky outside was a calm, late-summer blue, the kind of morning that almost feels like a promise. Our home was filled with the simple, quiet rhythm of routine—keys on the counter, my Bible tucked in my arms. But that peace shattered when my phone rang.

The number flashing across the screen was unfamiliar, from out of state. I let it buzz unanswered. Wrong number, I told myself. Spam, most likely. But the call came again. And again. Each time the sound pierced the quiet, my stomach clenched tighter. Finally, on the third attempt, I picked up.

Answering felt like stepping into another world.

On the other end was the husband of Gaylynn's Texas friend. His voice was steady and firm, but pulled taut like a wire close to snapping. And behind him, cutting through the line with terrifying clarity, were the sounds of Gaylynn's cries. Not cries, really—screams. Deep, raw, primal. They tore through the calm of my Sunday morning with a violence I cannot forget.

Over and over, she wailed the same words, her voice ragged and breaking: "THEY CAN'T FIND HER . . . THEY CAN'T FIND HER!"

My breath caught in my throat. Time slowed. My husband, sensing the stiffness in my body, stopped moving, his eyes fixed on me as though he, too, had felt the floor tilt beneath us. I pressed the phone tighter to my ear, my knees threatening to buckle.

I didn't even know who "her" was yet. But in my spirit, I knew.

The friend's husband tried to explain, his words tumbling out in fragments. A boating accident. Late the night before. Two boats colliding on a crowded lake, where holiday laughter had turned to panic in an instant. The impact had been violent, throwing everyone on board into the dark water. Among them were Gaylynn's middle daughter, her youngest daughter, her sister, and her brother-in-law.

The picture formed slowly, like glass shattering into pieces that cut as they fell. Her younger sister was in critical condition, airlifted to the nearest hospital. Her youngest daughter had somehow walked away with bruises and burns but no broken bones. And her brother-in-law was still among those unaccounted for.

Then came the words that explained Gaylynn's screams: Her middle daughter was also missing. Rescue teams were searching, but as the hours stretched, hope grew thin.

I clutched the phone, my hand slick with sweat. My husband stood close, steadying me with his presence, though neither of us knew what to say. There are no words when grief crashes in like that, unannounced and merciless.

For Gaylynn, thousands of miles away, the news struck like lightning. The friend at her side tried to keep her anchored, reminding her again and again that she had to stay calm. If she unraveled before boarding, the airline would never let her on that plane. This was her only way to her family, her only chance to face whatever truth awaited her. The thought of being stranded, powerless, while her daughter's fate hung in the balance. It was more than she could bear. This was a test not only of faith but of sheer will.

She screamed, she sobbed, she begged heaven for answers. And then, through sheer willpower, she steadied herself. The rupture inside her did not quiet, but she forced it behind a dam strong enough to get her through the motions of boarding. She gripped her friend's hand, gathered what little she carried, and braced herself to fly into the unthinkable.

Meanwhile, my husband and I shifted into urgency. Nothing else mattered but getting to her. We dropped everything—church plans, daily routine, the comfort of the ordinary—and began driving, my heart pounding with every mile. The Texas friend called us as she pieced together flight details, promising to get Gaylynn on the next plane, asking us to meet her at the airport and take her straight to the hospital where her sister had been admitted. We didn't hesitate.

The hours between those calls and her arrival stretched out like years. Waiting became its own kind of torment. We filled bags quickly, but then the car ride slowed time to a crawl. Every red light felt personal, every mile too long. My mind raced ahead to the hospital: What would we find? Who would we meet first? Would we have to tell Gaylynn the worst ourselves? I offered prayers under my breath, fragmented and unpolished, begging God to hold her until I could.

As her cousin, watching this unfold from a distance was agony. The helplessness pressed down like a boulder on my chest. I wanted nothing more than to shield her, to absorb even a fraction of the blow barreling toward her like a tidal wave. Instead, all I could do was prepare myself to be steady when she arrived—to be the calm in the wreckage when everything else was breaking apart.

When the moment finally came, we stood at the airport, my breath shallow as passengers trickled out, faces tired, eyes blank with travel. And then she appeared. I will never forget it. Gaylynn didn't walk so much as she stumbled forward, her face pale, her shoulders bowed under the gravity of anguish she hadn't yet been able to name. I wasn't convinced she even knew where she was. There was no dramatic scene, no wailing collapse. Just a mother whose body betrayed the battle raging within, each step evidence of a fight to remain upright.

The instant her eyes found me, her composure broke. She didn't need to say a word; I knew. I stepped toward her, gathering her in before she fell. Her body trembled in my arms, a mixture of exhaustion, fear, and sorrow pouring through her skin.

I led her out of the airport, through the blur of strangers and sterile corridors, into the heavy warmth of the day. We steadied her between us, loading her into the car, then drove directly to the hospital where her younger sister was being treated. Each breath felt laden, each movement slow, as though the world had transformed into a different dimension.

The hospital waiting room was already full when we arrived. The room smelled of disinfectant and burnt coffee, the kind that had been sitting too long on a warmer. The air was thick the moment we stepped inside, the oppressive sorrow already hanging in the halls. Voices carried low through the corridor, a hushed murmur that made the silence feel heavier. Time seemed suspended there, as though the walls themselves held their breath. This was where tragedy took root, where news broke hearts and prayers were lifted heavenward. Some people sat hunched in plastic chairs, their shoulders touching as though proximity alone could keep heartache at bay. Others paced in slow, restless circles, clutching Styrofoam cups or folded tissues. A TV mounted in the corner flickered silently, a surreal backdrop of weather reports and commercials against the heavy air of uncertainty.

Gaylynn's family waited inside, each face etched with anguish and disbelief. She entered as though carrying the remnants of all of them, and I knew in that moment the burst was complete. Nothing would ever be the same.

CHAPTER 13

AT THE CROSSROADS OF HOPE AND FEAR

"So do not fear, for I am with you; do not be dismayed, for I am your God. I will strengthen you and help you; I will uphold you with my righteous right hand."
— Isaiah 41:10

Friends, relatives, distant connections—all of them had gathered, each one bearing their own disbelief, their own helplessness. The room drifted with low voices and the occasional quiet sound of sobbing. People shifted in their seats and stared at the floor tiles as though the answers might appear there if they waited long enough. Gaylynn's birth father and uncle were already there, their presence quiet but grounding. We soon learned her mother, half brother, and half sister were on their way as well. It struck me, even in the fog of that day, how tragedy has a way of gathering people who have long been scattered. Here they came—pieces of Gaylynn's fractured family, each carrying their own histories, grievances, and regrets. Yet in that waiting room, none of it seemed to matter. Whatever distance had lived between them before was suspended, if only briefly, by the urgency of not knowing.

Unsure of how long we'd be there, I slipped out long enough to book a two-room suite at a nearby hotel. It was the most practical thing I could do in the middle of the upheaval: carve out a place where we could retreat, even if rest seemed impossible.

Most of us stayed close to the hospital, anxiously waiting for any update about the missing passengers from the boat, Gaylynn's middle daughter among them. Though visitation was tightly controlled, I managed to see Gaylynn's younger sister, who had been in the accident, for a short time. The sight of her shook me. She was in excruciating pain, her body bruised and broken, her face etched with both physical agony and emotional devastation. She described the crash in fragments, her voice weak. She said it sounded like a bomb had gone off at impact—an explosion so sudden and violent it split the night open. Darkness had swallowed everything, making it impossible to see who was in the water. She remembered only the confusion: bodies scattered, voices crying out, water closing over heads, silence where there should have been life.

When Gaylynn entered her sister's room, I was with her, uncertain how the reunion would unfold. It was the first time they had been face-to-face in years, after a relationship that had once been inseparable but had long since fractured. Watching their connection dissolve over the years had always been heartbreaking for me. I couldn't help but remember them as girls—finishing each other's sentences, clinging to one another against the shadows of their childhood. To see them now, separated not by distance but by silence, was almost more than I could bear. The bond of childhood seemed like a faded photograph. Their words to each other were few, their eyes averted. Gaylynn's hand brushed the blanket but didn't reach for her sister, the gap between them wider than the hospital bed. It was a tragedy layered on top of tragedy, and my heart broke all over again.

Back in the waiting room, the tension was unbearable. People moved in and out, whispering updates no one wanted to hear. Gaylynn could not sit still. She paced the length of the room like a caged animal, the grief and fear inside her demanding motion. When anyone tried to console her, she snapped. The words were sharp, her tone laced with desperation. Her footsteps echoed against the linoleum floor, piercing and uneven, each turn punctuated by a deep breath or muttered word. Her hands twisted together, knuckles whitening, as if even her fingers couldn't contain the upheaval inside her. Watching her, I knew her actions were not only from exhaustion; this mother's body was simply carrying more grief than it could hold. Some in the room averted their eyes, unsure whether to reach out or retreat. The grief inside her needed motion, needed release, and the confined walls of the waiting room became too small to contain it. At one point, hospital staff approached, their concern not only for her but for the others around her. I could see it in their eyes; they were debating whether to remove her.

I crossed the room and reached for her arm. She turned on me, too, lashing out. But I held firm. My words came out hard, sharper than I intended, but necessary: "You have to get control of yourself. If you don't, they're going to make you leave. I won't let that happen. But you need to stop yelling at people."

It was like splashing cold water on her face. She froze, her chest heaving, and then slowly, almost reluctantly, she sat. For the first time since her plane landed, she stayed in one place. The upheaval inside her didn't disappear, but it quieted enough to let her endure the hours that followed.

That evening, I convinced her to leave the hospital with us. It wasn't easy; she fought me every step of the way, unwilling to be separated from the last thread of connection she had to her missing daughter. But exhaustion had hollowed her out, and eventually she relented. We had dinner, though none of us tasted it, then retreated to our hotel room. I promised her we would return first thing in the morning. Still, I don't think she slept at all that night. How could she? She was living every mother's worst nightmare—knowing her child was out there somewhere, perhaps hurt, perhaps gone, and powerless to change it.

The next morning, as the sun rose over a world that felt foreign, we returned to the hospital. The hours dragged like years. Coffee cups emptied and refilled, phones buzzed with updates that never satisfied. Some people prayed aloud, their words breaking in the middle, while others bowed their heads in silence. I found myself praying under my breath with fragments of scripture, not always with conviction but because I needed something to hold on to. Time in that room wasn't measured by clocks but by the weight of each unanswered question.

Finally, the first update came. One of the missing had been found. Deceased. My heart lodged in my throat. But it wasn't her daughter. It was another passenger. Relief and devastation collided in the same breath. Gaylynn's body slumped with the tiniest exhale; her daughter was still unaccounted for. But then the guilt came, unspoken yet heavy: Another family's loss was now her borrowed reprieve. Every update became a double-edged sword, cutting one way with grief and the other with fragile hope.

The days blurred together, a haze of waiting rooms and updates that were never enough. Within a few days, two more bodies were recovered. One was Gaylynn's brother-in-law—the captain of the boat, her younger sister's husband. The other was her daughter's friend who had joined them for the long weekend on the lake. When the news came that her brother-in-law and the friend had been found, the room split into grief again. Some sobbed openly; others went still, staring at the floor as though it might explain the unexplainable. Gaylynn sat rigid, her fists clenched on her knees. Each discovery chipped away at hope, yet she refused to let it collapse completely. Each announcement tore through the room like a blade. Faces crumpled, cries echoed, prayers pressed into clenched fists.

Yet through it all, there was still no word about Gaylynn's daughter. Search crews pressed on, combing the riverbank, dragging the water, sending out divers and boats. Every ring of a phone jolted us upright. Every footstep in the hallway made our hearts race. We prayed in fragments, desperate petitions for a miracle. Perhaps she had made it to the shore, possibly she was unconscious in a hospital under a different name. We prayed because it was all we had left.

But the silence stretched on.

Eventually, we had to leave. As impossible as it felt to tear Gaylynn away from the hospital—the place that still tethered her to her daughter—we had no choice. Staying in a hotel indefinitely was not possible, and her younger sister's recovery was expected to be long. The decision was like pulling her back from the edge of an abyss she was determined to cling to. Her resistance was fierce, but finally, broken by exhaustion and the insistence of those around her, she agreed. Her eyes pleaded even when her words fell silent. Every step toward the door felt like a betrayal, as though walking away meant abandoning her daughter. I held her arm firmly, not because she needed guidance but because I knew she might turn and bolt back at any moment.

We drove home in silence. The world outside the car window blurred—a contradiction of normalcy, people pumping gas, walking dogs, living their lives, while ours had stopped. My hands rested in my lap as I fought the urge to call my family, just to hear their voices. Grief has a way of making every ordinary act feel sacred, every breath of your loved ones a gift you don't deserve to take for granted.

Nothing about this grief made sense. It never would.

As the days stretched into nights and the search dragged on, the hospital became both a refuge and a torment. It was the only place that tethered Gaylynn to her daughter, yet every hour without answers felt like another cut into her spirit. Leaving was unthinkable, yet staying changed nothing. When we finally pulled her away, her body was present, but her soul remained at the water's edge.

What none of us could know then was that the gravity of loss was only the beginning. Even as she clung to hope for her daughter, another shadow was forming—one that would soon demand every ounce of courage left within her. What awaited was not only grief, but a battle for her very life.

CHAPTER 14

WHEN WAITING BECOMES ITS OWN GRIEF

"Waiting is not empty time. It is the space where faith and fear wrestle for the heart."

The first few days at home with Gaylynn were drenched in sorrow. She moved like someone caught in quicksand, every step pulling her deeper into despair. Most of the time, she stayed in bed, the heaviness of loss pinning her to the mattress. The house itself seemed to absorb her sorrow. The blinds stayed drawn, sunlight barely piercing the room where she lay in bed. I tiptoed through the hallways, every sound magnified, afraid that even the sound of my shuffling feet might disturb her fragile rest. At night I lay awake listening for movement, worried she might slip out unnoticed or that despair might swallow her whole. She slept for hours on end, rising only to nibble at food or to check her messages, her phone clutched like a lifeline to news that never came.

I hovered close. I didn't want to leave her alone, not in that state. Every hour, I checked on her, watching for signs that her despair might take her somewhere I couldn't reach. She promised me she wouldn't harm herself, and I believed her, but promises made in heartache always carry fragility. I watched her closely, not because I doubted her word, but because sorrow can speak one way in daylight and another in the quiet hours of night. My mind was constantly running—planning meals she might actually eat, watching for signs of life in her eyes, listening for the faintest shift in her voice. I prayed over her under my breath, asking God to carry her through when my own strength was not enough. Still, she insisted she had made a vow: She would not leave our hometown until they brought her daughter home.

My heart ached for her. Once again, I found myself at a loss for how to comfort her in the face of pain so sharp it cut past words. I could sit with her, pray over her, hold her hand when she let me—but sorrow of that magnitude belongs to no one else. It is a wilderness no one can enter except the one who has lost a child. All I knew to do was remain steady, praying constantly for her strength, for her peace, for God's nearness in a darkness that felt impenetrable.

Days turned into weeks. Weeks turned into months. Still, there was no word.

The search for Gaylynn's daughter had moved far beyond the official investigation. At first, family members relayed updates from the authorities—boats scanning the river, divers combing the depths, teams walking the shorelines. As the silence stretched, others joined. Friends, neighbors, and strangers who had never met Gaylynn but had heard the story began showing up. Flyers were distributed. Volunteers came from other counties, even from other states, compelled by compassion to join the effort. People combed riverbanks with flashlights, launched boats at dawn, and pinned flyers to gas station windows. Some came with trained dogs; others brought nothing but willing hands and heavy hearts. I was humbled by the compassion of strangers who had never met Gaylynn or her daughter but still showed up. For a while, the community moved as though bound together by a single heartbeat; one mother's missing child had become everyone's burden. Yet each search ended in silence. With every fruitless day, hope became harder to hold, and the ache in Gaylynn's eyes deepened. Despite the manpower, despite the prayers, every search ended the same way: empty.

Watching Gaylynn live inside that uncertainty was excruciating. She balanced on a knife's edge—hope one moment, despair the next.

Each day brought no answers, and the silence stretched into a hollow stillness that seeped into the very walls of my house.

After several months of this suspended grief, something in Gaylynn shifted. Perhaps it was exhaustion from waiting, or the need to claw back some small measure of control, but she decided she had to do something. She went to her mother's house and retrieved her old bike—the same one she had pedaled as though it could take her away from sorrow. She found a part-time job for the Christmas season, close enough to my house that she could ride the bike to work.

The job was simple retail, nothing glamorous, but it gave her structure, a reason to rise each morning, and a place to be other than her bed. It also gave her a little independence. Watching her pedal through town, scarf trailing in the wind, I glimpsed a flicker of the old Gaylynn—the one who had always pushed forward, who refused to stay down for long. That old bike carried her more than just across town; it carried her into a fragile sense of normalcy.

But heartache is never far away.

One afternoon, while at work, my phone rang. Gaylynn was on the other end, hysterical. Her sobs were so deep I could barely make out the words. My stomach dropped, convinced this was *the* call . . . that they had found her daughter. I rushed home, heart pounding.

When I arrived, she had crumpled on the couch, shaking, her face streaked with tears. "They stole my bike," she choked out between sobs. For a moment, the absurdity of it almost made me laugh in disbelief. A stolen bike hardly seemed like the thing to unravel her. But in that moment, I understood. It wasn't about the bicycle. It was about what the bicycle represented: liberation, a small slice of independence, a rhythm to her days. When it vanished, the little ground she had gained was snatched from her. Her sobs that afternoon carried the sting of so many other losses, spilling out over the handlebars of a simple old bike. She was living with raw edges exposed, emotions stretched so thin that even the smallest loss could send her crashing.

When she finally calmed enough to explain, the story became even more surreal. A close male friend of hers had been renting part of her house in Belize. The housekeeper there had called, frantic, saying the tenant wasn't responding. Gaylynn instructed her to break in. What she found was horrifying: The man had been dead for nearly a week, discovered lifeless on the floor.

Gaylynn had received that call while at work. Already reeling, she went to leave and then discovered her bike was gone. That was what broke her completely—not simply the theft of a possession but the piling on of one more thing, one more loss, one more blow on a spirit already staggering.

I held her as she sobbed, reminding myself that pain magnifies everything. To anyone else, a stolen bike might be a nuisance. To her, it was one more reminder that life was spiraling beyond her control.

In time, Gaylynn decided she could not keep living in my house. She didn't want to feel like a burden. She needed space of her own. Around that time, she had begun doing yoga again, trying to move her body and find quiet in her mind. There she met a man who noticed her sorrow and treated her with compassion. When he learned she was looking for a place to stay, he offered her a room in his home. All she had to do was cover the cost of her food.

With the money she had saved from her seasonal job, Gaylynn accepted. It wasn't far from us, but it gave her a measure of independence. At first, it was only a room rental, but over time, the relationship deepened. I wanted to believe this was a turning point for her, that kindness could knit some of her wounds together. Still, I couldn't help but wonder if the timing was too fragile, if she was leaning on someone else before she had the chance to stand on her own. Yet even with my reservations, I could see how his presence steadied her, how she laughed a little easier, how she began to imagine a life beyond constant waiting. She began working for him as an assistant in his business. He bought her an old used car, freeing her from reliance on others to get around. Together they made small plans—weekend trips, business travel, time away from the grief-soaked air of home.

I didn't fully know what to make of it. Part of me was relieved she had someone kind at her side, someone who was easing her days. Another part of me wondered if it was too soon, too fragile, too much for a woman who was still unraveling inside. But I said little. She was determined to keep moving forward, and who was I to take that from her?

Months later, Gaylynn decided she needed to return to Belize. Her house had been left unattended after the death of her friend, and there were matters she needed to resolve. I worried, of course. Travel felt dangerous, not because of the place but because of her fragile state. Still, I was reassured that her new boyfriend would be going with her. They left together and stayed for several weeks, tending to the house, trying to tie off the loose ends she had left when tragedy first struck.

When they returned, they barely paused before planning another trip. Early that summer, they went to Idaho, then on to Mexico for adventurous hiking and sightseeing. This time they were joined by a group of young women Gaylynn had been mentoring—a glimpse of her heart for others breaking through the heaviness of her own pain. She assured me she'd be back in a few weeks. She told me not to worry.

But I did.

In the weeks before she left, Gaylynn had been complaining of not feeling well. She'd brushed it off, attributing it to stress. And who could argue? The mourning, the memorials, the endless waiting for news of her daughter—it would have been enough to break the body as well as the spirit. Still, something in her complaints unsettled me. A tone in her voice, a color in her face, small signs that there was something deeper.

I tried to convince myself it was nothing, that her body was simply tired from carrying too much for too long. But deep down, I couldn't shake the feeling that we were on the edge of another trial. I prayed I was wrong, that her body only needed rest after so much sorrow. But in the quiet of my heart, I felt the warning settle in my chest like a knot, an undertow that told me something darker was already moving beneath the surface.

What I didn't know then was how harsh that battle would be, or how much more it would ask of her.

CHAPTER 15

THE UNSEEN BATTLE

"The spirit is willing, but the flesh is weak."—Mark 14:38

In hindsight, Gaylynn now understands she should have sought medical attention even before the death of her daughter. For many years, she had experienced bouts of not feeling well—aches that lingered, fatigue that clung to her like a second skin, stomach troubles she brushed off as stress or the cost of living a full life. She was always too busy, too strong-willed, too determined to be slowed down. Whatever it was, she told herself, could wait until later.

But later never came.

It wasn't until she traveled to Mexico for a yoga retreat that everything came to the surface in a way she could no longer ignore. Surrounded by a group of young women she was mentoring and the man who had befriended her and recently become her companion, Gaylynn was supposed to be experiencing peace, restoration, and even joy. The trip had been planned for months, an escape—a reprieve from the heaviness at home. Instead, her body betrayed her.

She couldn't keep anything down. Food, even water, brought wave after wave of vomiting. Her belly swelled as though something inside was pressing outward, leaving her unable to find relief. She admitted she couldn't use the bathroom; her voice strained with discomfort. One of the women gently suggested she see a doctor, concern lacing her voice. Gaylynn shook her head, brushing it aside. "It's just stress," she insisted. "When I get home, if it's not better, I'll go." She said it with the stubbornness that had carried her through so much of life—the insistence that she could push through whatever came her way.

And push through she did.

They continued the retreat, moving from yoga mats to hiking trails, snorkeling coves, and swimming under the Mexican sun. On the surface, she joined in—stretching, laughing, floating in the turquoise water. But those closest to her could see the facade was starting to crumble. Her smiles didn't quite reach her eyes. Her movements slowed. Her body, always so full of energy and life, carried a strain that was impossible to ignore. While others floated easily in the water, she lay back on the sand, the scent of salt and sunscreen sharp in the air, her stomach roiling with every breath.

At the end of a long hike to a large, popular ruin, the disguise gave way. The day had been grueling, the sun unrelenting, the trail winding and steep. Gaylynn tried to keep up, but by the time they reached the top, her strength failed. She doubled over, clutching her stomach, her face pale and strained. This time, one of the young women traveling with her insisted: "You need to go to the hospital." The others hovered close, their laughter muted now, replaced by worried glances.

Her body was wracked with nausea. She couldn't eat. She couldn't drink. She could hardly force herself to move. And yet, Gaylynn's instinct was still to minimize, to push forward, to insist she would be fine.

Those of us back home didn't yet know the full extent of what was happening in Mexico. We only knew that Gaylynn's calls and messages carried hints of exhaustion she couldn't quite hide. When she returned, she would share more, but even then, she cloaked it with determination. "I'll get it checked out," she promised. "But not yet. Not today."

At the time, I chalked it up to grief. Of course her body was weary. Of course she was struggling. Stress explains a thousand symptoms, and horrifying loss explains a thousand more.

But deep down, something unsettled me. There was a tone in her voice, a slackness in her face, that I couldn't shake. My prayers for her evolved subtly during those days. I still prayed for peace, for strength, for the return of her daughter. But I also prayed for her body, for healing in ways I didn't yet have words for.

She, of course, wouldn't admit how bad it was. Gaylynn had always been the one to push through, to prove herself stronger than the obstacles in her path. That determination had carried her through abusive relationships, through financial struggle, through devastating loss. But the body is not infinite. It signals quietly at first, then it warns, and finally it demands.

Mexico was the warning.

None of us yet understood that her body was signaling a far heavier truth. At the time, she seemed to be suffering from sheer exhaustion, stress, perhaps even the consequence of trying to keep too busy while her heart was breaking. But in hindsight, the signs were already there, written in the way her body faltered on that trip.

I think of it now as the shadow before the breaking. We could not see it clearly then, but it was already gathering, already casting its outline across her days.

What we didn't know—what Gaylynn herself refused to imagine—was that another enemy had already taken shape inside her, an enemy that would demand every ounce of her courage in the months and years ahead.

Even in darkness, the flame endured.

ACT IV

THE BREAKING POINT

"We are hard pressed on every side, but not crushed;
perplexed, but not in despair; persecuted, but not abandoned;
struck down, but not destroyed."— 2 Corinthians 4:8-9

By the time Gaylynn reached this chapter of her story, her life already bore the marks of wounds too deep to count: A childhood splintered by abuse. A sister once inseparable, now distant. Marriages that left her bruised in body and spirit. Daughters who each were disconnected from her and carried their own stories, the strain of a fractured family pressing down on them all. And then, the unthinkable—the daughter she lost in an instant, her body still missing, her absence stretching on like an open wound.

Every fracture, every heartbreak had carved lines of sorrow and resilience into Gaylynn's life. She had always found a way forward, even when the path was jagged. The girl I had known since childhood—the one who was strong, spirited, unafraid to stare down what others avoided—was still there. But the fortitude that had carried her this far was about to be tested in a way no one could prepare for.

Her daughter was still gone. Her family remained scattered, some close, others estranged. And just when it seemed her spirit could bear no more, her body began to falter, the warning signs surfacing in ways she could no longer dismiss. This part of her story was not about one struggle but two: grief that seared the heart, and illness that threatened her very life. Sorrow and illness together became a force no one could outrun.

CHAPTER 16

TORN BETWEEN MOURNING AND SURVIVAL

"Strength does not come from what you can do. It comes from overcoming the things you once thought you couldn't."
— *Anonymous*

Gaylynn had pushed through as long as she could, but her body finally forced her hand. In Mexico, after days of vomiting, swelling, and sheer exhaustion, she knew she couldn't wait any longer. She called an ambulance for herself and was admitted to a local emergency room. The ambulance ride jolted her through unfamiliar streets, sirens wailing in a language that wasn't her own. The hospital smelled faintly of diesel fuel drifting in from outside. Nurses spoke in hurried Spanish, their words a blur that she half understood, half guessed by their faces. She felt very far from home, a stranger in a body that was abandoning her, in a place where she didn't belong. For three days, doctors ran a battery of tests, prodding and scanning as she drifted in and out of restless sleep.

On the third day, a doctor entered her room, pulled up a chair, and sat on the edge of her bed. Her face carried the kind of gravity that said everything before she spoke. Later, Gaylynn confided that she knew something was terribly wrong from the look in her eyes. Glancing down, the doctor picked lint from her pants before she spoke. Gaylynn braced herself. Even before the word "cancer" left her lips, Gaylynn felt the floor disappear beneath her. The word itself seemed almost secondary to the gravity written across her face.

She explained that Gaylynn had a very large tumor and told her the words no one is ever ready to hear: colon cancer. She needed emergency surgery, she said, and the cost would be twenty-two thousand dollars—due immediately.

In that moment, Gaylynn's world shifted into something unrecognizable. Still reeling from the sorrow of her missing daughter, she was now faced with a life-threatening diagnosis far from home. She picked up her phone, hands trembling, and called her younger sister. Then she called her dear friend in Texas, whose steady presence had carried her through so many trials.

Thanks to her friend's medical connections and her insistence that Gaylynn return to the States, a plan was set into motion. Arrangements were made for a flight out of Mexico the very next morning. Gaylynn's youngest daughter, an ICU nurse, met her at the airport and drove her directly to UCLA hospital in Los Angeles, where she was immediately admitted.

At UCLA, further tests confirmed the severity of her condition. She was moved to the oncology ward. When I spoke with her by phone, her voice carried the same spark it always had—joking, laughing, deflecting. But I knew better. Beneath her lighthearted words was something heavier. When she finally told me about the diagnosis, I was shocked. My first reaction was confusion, even anger. Why would God allow this? I had already asked God why once before, when Gaylynn's daughter was gone in an instant. Now here I was again, pleading for answers that didn't come. My Bible lay open on the table, but the words felt like stones in my mouth. Faith was no less real, but it was raw and fragile. I wasn't doubting God's existence; I was doubting His mercy. After everything she had already endured—the trauma of her childhood, her broken family, the unbearable loss of her daughter—why now this? Why this ordeal on top of all the others?

That night, Gaylynn's voice was tired but steady. She didn't linger long on details; instead, she ended the call the way she often did when she needed me most. "Can you get on your Batphone to God for me?" she asked, her humor shading the heaviness. It was her short-hand for prayer, her way of asking me to intercede when she couldn't carry the words herself. I promised her I would, and when the line went silent, I stayed there praying long into the night.

I prayed constantly, and my faith never wavered. I pleaded for answers, for some explanation I could hold on to. I needed something. Some reassurance that she would be okay. Over and over, though, the words of Psalm 46:10 pressed into me: "Be still, and know that I am God." It was not the answer I wanted, but it was the only one I received.

During those weeks, Gaylynn's dear friend from Texas flew out to see her. She carefully reviewed Gaylynn's medical records and went over the test results. While she was there, Gaylynn underwent a stomach drainage procedure. The doctors removed liters of thick white fluid. Her friend's face fell as she realized the seriousness of what was happening. She told Gaylynn later that she had never known anyone to survive after that much infection had been drained. She began calling Gaylynn's friends and family, urging them to visit quickly and say their goodbyes. Gaylynn's body had gone septic, she said, and it was only a matter of time before her organs shut down.

But I knew differently. I had been praying steadily since her time in Mexico, asking God for clarity. Again and again, I asked whether I should rush to her side, whether time was short. And each time, I sensed the same quiet proclamation: "I am not finished with her yet. I have more for her to do."

Gaylynn remained in the hospital for four weeks. The doctors' immediate goal was simply to stabilize her, to get her strong enough to be discharged. They explained that once home, she would need palliative care. Yet there was another cruel obstacle: Gaylynn had no health insurance. The hospital staff made it clear that their treatment options would be limited because of it. Another battle, stacked on the ones she was already fighting.

Her time at UCLA carried another layer of anguish, one that pressed beneath the surface of everything else she faced. While still in the oncology ward, she marked the one-year anniversary of her daughter's death. Her nurses, who had come to know her story, helped her create a small altar in her room. The nurses brought what they could—flickering battery candles, a white cloth draped over a bedside table, a vase with a single flower. They gathered her photos, taping one above the bed where she could see her daughter's face each morning.

The candles' silent glow softened the sterile edges of the room, a quiet testimony that even in suffering, love could be honored. It was a sacred act of defiance, a way for her to keep vigil for her daughter even as her own body betrayed her. Amid the sterile walls, she carved out a small slice of holy ground.

Gaylynn confided in me years later that she had known the truth long before anyone confirmed it. The moment she got the call that her daughter was missing, she said she couldn't feel her anymore—like a mother who suddenly senses an emptiness where life used to be. It wasn't denial or hope that followed, but the quiet knowing of a mother's broken heart.

Eventually, she was discharged. The man who had once been her romantic partner, now a companion and steady friend, drove her home. But by mid-September, her health had deteriorated further. Her skin was pale, almost ashen. Walking even short distances left her breathless.

Finally, she found an oncologist willing to treat her. He reviewed her scans and delivered the words she dreaded but already knew: stage 4 colon cancer. A large tumor had been found in her intestine. The doctor explained it directly: She had a completely obstructing sigmoid mass, and her bowel had already perforated. Without aggressive chemotherapy, he warned, she had only weeks, perhaps months, to live. I sat with those words, stunned by how casually they seemed to measure a life in weeks.

The doctor made no promises of a permanent recovery. "This is not curable," he said. "Our goal is to control the disease for as long as possible."

Gaylynn hesitated because of fear of the unknown. We had many conversations, prayed a lot, and she ultimately began treatment.

Chemotherapy hit her like a wrecking ball. Within days of her first treatment, she was sicker than she had ever been in her life. Nothing stayed down. Even water came back up in waves. Her pounds dropped rapidly. She survived on a single protein shake a day, her body too weak to digest much else. The sharp chemical smell of chemo lingered in the room, clinging to her skin and clothes, impossible to escape. Her hair thinned, strands left behind on the pillow like fragile reminders of the fight. She had always been known for her long, thick, dark hair, and the sight of it thinning startled me each time. She never lost it all, but even that small change felt like a cruel reminder of what the cancer had taken. She eventually cut her hair short to minimize the appearance of the diminishing locks. She was too tired to cry, too worn to rage; her quiet carried more than words ever could. The medications to manage pain and nausea left her dazed, barely awake. Whenever I visited, she mostly slept, her once-bright energy swallowed by fatigue and pharmaceuticals. The torment of her daughter's absence clung to her even here, woven through the sickness in her body.

The oncologist had recommended twelve rounds of chemotherapy. Gaylynn made it through six. Each treatment carved more out of her, leaving her skeletal, hollow-eyed, too frail to endure further. By November, she barely weighed 110 pounds.

At her seventh scheduled treatment, she planned to refuse. She was done. But the clinic required routine bloodwork before every appointment, and this time her results raised alarms. Her oncologist sent her immediately to the emergency room.

There, she met the doctor she would later call her "angel surgeon." He admitted her straightaway for more testing. A few days later, he came with unexpected news: The tumor had shrunk enough to be surgically removed. Against all odds, the same body that had betrayed her was now showing a glimmer of promise.

Her oncologist had doubted she would ever reach this point, but the surgeon saw differently. For the first time in months, Gaylynn's eyes lit up with something I had not seen since before her daughter's disappearance: expectation. I understood why she called him her angel. His voice carried a steadiness that no other doctor had given her. Where others saw only an ending, he spoke of a chance. It was the first time anyone had dared suggest her life was not already written in its final chapter. Hope, faint and flickering, returned to her eyes in that moment.

And true to her nature, she grabbed hold of it. She had defied the odds before. She was ready to do it again.

fax

Date of Service: 09

Patient Name: Gaylynn
Date of Birth: 07/2 , Age:
MRN.
Attending Physicia (Hematology/Oncology)
Referring Physician MD (Internal Medicine)

Dear Dr

Thank you very much for kindly referring Mrs. for medical oncology evaluation and treatment for her advanced colon cancer.

Colon Cancer
  Date of Diagnosis: 8/16/.
  Post-menopausal
  Stage: T4aNxM1b=**Stage IV** (Large completely obstructing sigmoid mass with perforation and pelvic abscess; CT scan:
  Multiple peritoneal and omental nodules; no distant mets)
  Location: **Sigmoid colon**
  Phenotype/Genotype
  Histology: **Adenocarcinoma**
  Grade 2/3
  CEA level
  KRAS: Positive Mutation; NRAS neg, BRAF neg, AKT1 neg, PIK3CA neg. Her-2/neu: pending
  MSI: 4 MMR genes normal (neg)
  Liquid Biopsy NGS
  My Risk Profile
  Line of Therapy
  1. Dual sigmoid colon stents (8/16/19), I.R. drainage of 2 Liter 17 cm abscess (8/21/19)
  2. FOLFOX/Avastin (pending)

HPI
This -year-old white female was in Mexico teaching yoga when she developed abdominal pain which continued for a week becoming more severe until she went to a physician and had a colonoscopy which revealed an obstructing tumor in the sigmoid colon. She was advised to have emergency surgery but instead she immediately flew to Los Angeles and her daughter who is an ICU nurse drove her to UCLA emergency room where she was admitted on August 15 and stayed until September 9. Although we do not have the pathology report, the records state that she had another colonoscopy done on August 16 and had two stents placed because of an obstructing sigmoid mass. Biopsies revealed a grade 2 adenocarcinoma. A CT Scan reportedly showed peritoneal nodules as well as nodules behind the uterine body and a non-specific right upper lobe lung nodule. On August 20 a CT Scan showed a large rim enhancing irregular anterior pelvic fluid collection that measured 17 cm thought to be an abscess due to a prior contained colon perforation due to the obstruction. The scan showed the obstructing mass and the omental nodules. There was also distal or terminal ileum mild fluid and gas distention of the small bowel loops in the right lower quadrant thought to be due to extrinsic compression by the large pelvic fluid collection. There were serosal peritoneal implants seen in the pelvis and the largest was adjacent to the rectum. There were also implants ventral to the rectum and posterior to the uterine body and diffuse peritoneal studding. There was also mild bilateral hydronephrosis with distal ureter compressed in the pelvis b the large fluid collection. She had this fluid collection drained of about 2000 ml of pus and then a pigtail catheter was placed for ongoing drainage and her symptoms significantly improved with this drainage. The surgeons were planning to place a diverting colostomy but then this was cancelled after the fluid collection was drained by interventional radiology. She was also treated with IV antibiotics and has time went on she had decreasing distention and increased ability to pass flatus with relief of her abdominal discomfort. The cytology was negative on this fluid collection. She continued on antibiotics until August 26 and her white count dropped and eventually she was able to stop the antibiotics and it was thought the infection had resolved. She has not received any specific treatment for the cancer so far. Since her discharge she has continued to have problems with vomiting a lot, although that had improved significantly in the hospital when she had her medicines adjusted and was getting Marinol twice a day 10 mg and taking Compazine. Her pain was also controlled with Morphine Sulfate Extended Release 15 mg every 12 hours, but she did not have any improvement in her nausea with the Zofran. She has continued to have small stools which are loose about twice a day. She has continued to have pain all of the time now. She has run out of her Morphine Sulfate Immediate Release 15 mg which she had been using to control the pain. She states that Phenergan had worked better for her in the past but t works better than Zofran, which does not work at all. She is also using some CBD oil applied to her abdomen.

What the doctors saw, what God already knew: stage 4 colon cancer.

CHAPTER 17

THE COURAGE TO FIGHT

"But Jesus came and touched them. 'Get up,' he said. 'Don't be afraid.'"— Matthew 17:7

Gaylynn's surgery stretched on through the long, dragging hours of the day and into the fading light of early evening. The waiting room felt clinical and cold, fluorescent lights buzzing faintly overhead. I sat stiffly on the rigid chair, trying to mold myself into comfort. I pretended to read, prayed without stopping, and fidgeted in my chair to ease the ache in my back. I tried to lose myself in my book, but the words swam together, unreadable against the pounding of my thoughts. Across the room, someone chuckled faintly at the sitcom rerun playing on the muted television, and the sound struck me as absurd. How could anyone laugh when life hung by a thread in the operating room just beyond these walls?

Every detail of that room imprinted itself on my memory—the scuffed floor tiles, the relentless flicker of the overhead light, the coffee machine in the corner that hissed and sputtered but never produced anything drinkable. Time seemed to fold in on itself there, minutes dragging like hours. I remember staring at the hands of the clock, willing them to move faster, but also dreading what the next minute might bring.

Her mother was there too, her face drawn and tired, her eyes shadowed with worry she rarely voiced. A mother's anguish shows plainly in her face, and in hers I saw a lifetime of heartache in a single afternoon. Gaylynn's half sister joined us for a while, though their relationship remained fragile. Blood ties, however strained, still carried a shadow; she felt compelled to be there, offering what support she could muster, even amid unresolved wounds. Their presence was complicated—fraught with history—but for those hours, history was set aside. We were bound not by resolution but by the shared terror of not knowing.

In that room, I became the quiet center for us all, holding my faith close like a shield against the creeping fear. It wasn't a role I sought, but I felt the burden of it all the same. For most of my life, I had been the one others turned to in moments like this, the one with steady hands and a prayer always ready. That day was no different. Their eyes drifted toward me in moments of stillness, as though my steadiness could anchor them. I prayed not only for Gaylynn but for the resolve to keep holding steady for those around me. I thought of Gaylynn's familiar request to "get on the Batphone to God," and it echoed in me as I prayed. She couldn't speak the words herself, not from that hospital bed, but I carried them for her. I prayed as though I could hold the line open until she was strong enough to pick it up again. Faith in moments like that isn't triumphant; it's fragile. It wavers between unspoken confidence and desperate pleading. I prayed the same lines over and over, sometimes with conviction, other times only to keep from unraveling. Faith became less about certainty and more about refusing to let go.

The hours dragged on with agonizing slowness. Each time the door swung open, my heart caught, only to fall again when it was just another nurse passing through. We exchanged nervous glances, but mostly we sat in a hush, the strain of waiting pressing into every corner of that bleak room.

At last, the surgeon appeared. His face was tired but serious, his eyes holding the gravity of what he had just endured. When we locked eyes, he walked directly toward me. His initial heavy sigh and silence was deafening. Once he steadied himself, he began his explanation: The surgery had been incredibly complicated. The tumor was large and had perforated her colon, spilling waste into her abdominal cavity—a dangerous situation that prolonged the operation. The cleanup alone had required painstaking care to stave off infection.

He went on to explain that they had removed the tumor and a large portion of her colon. But the damage was so extensive that they had to place a colostomy bag on her left side. It was likely to be permanent—a reality we could hardly process. I knew how she valued her independence, how proud she was of her body that had carried her through so much. To imagine her waking to this new reality, a bag strapped to her side, felt like such an intrusion. It was more than a medical device; it was a thief, stealing not only her health but a part of her dignity. Later, when the reality of the colostomy bag settled in, I felt my breath catch. This was not a temporary measure. It was a daily, permanent reminder of what the cancer had stolen. I couldn't imagine how she would reconcile the life she had lived—active, independent, resolute—with this new reality. But if I knew anything about Gaylynn, it was that she would find a way. All we could cling to in that moment was the one undeniable truth: She was alive.

In the days that followed, Gaylynn was moved to the intensive care unit and placed on life support. Visiting hours were brief, restricted to one person at a time. The ICU was a world of its own: dim, impersonal, filled with the steady buzz of machines and the relentless beeping of monitors. The lights in the ICU were dimmed low, a perpetual twilight meant to keep patients calm. Nurses moved with a quiet urgency, their faces unreadable behind masks. I pressed my hand against the cool glass, my reflection superimposed over Gaylynn's frail body. It was jarring—to see myself whole and strong while she lay diminished, every breath dependent on a machine.

Peering through the glass, I saw her body connected to tubes and wires, her chest rising and falling with the aid of a ventilator. The ICU smelled of bleach and machinery, every breath punctuated by the hiss of ventilators and the steady beep of monitors. I pressed my hand against the glass, quietly saying her name, as if my voice could thread its way past tubes and sedation to reach her spirit. The Gaylynn I knew—the one who filled a room with laughter and presence—was hidden beneath layers of medical equipment. I had to remind myself she was still there, still fighting, even if I couldn't see it. Though I struggled to reconcile the fragility before me with the warrior she had become, I never let go of the belief that God's promise was bigger than the circumstances.

Seeing her so vulnerable—frail, weakened, a machine breathing for her—was almost too much to bear. And yet, doubt lingered. Despite my belief in God's promises, creeping fears gnawed at the edges of my heart. Could she really pull through this? Could her body endure so much? I kept envisioning the moment she'd awaken, cracking one of her trademark jokes and demanding to get out of bed. That image became my prayer: that her laughter would return, that her stubborn will would carry her through.

Days that felt like weeks finally passed, and then came the first sign of victory. Gaylynn was taken off the ventilator and moved into a regular hospital room. Slowly, glimmers of the old Gaylynn emerged. During one visit, she surprised me by asking for a Filet-O-Fish from McDonald's—a simple, almost childlike request that felt like a spark of her spirit breaking through the haze. That request was more than a craving; it was a declaration. It was her way of saying, "I'm still here. I still get to choose." Watching her take those first tentative bites made me feel like I could finally take a breath. It wasn't about the sandwich. It was about the spark of defiance in her eyes, the proof that her spirit had not been crushed.

Later, she confided in me about what had happened while she was on life support. Amid the mechanical rhythms of the ICU, she said she heard a voice—gentle but commanding—speaking into the depths of her spirit: *Get up. It's not your time.* She believed it was God, urging her to hold on. With the words came a promise: Her daughter would be found and brought home on July 4.

When she shared that story with me, there was no hesitation in her voice. It wasn't a dream, she insisted. It wasn't the fog of sedation. It was God, speaking into the deepest part of her being. The way she described it left no room for doubt; her eyes shone with the certainty of someone who had touched eternity and returned with a message.

One afternoon, a close friend visited her. Their quiet conversation was interrupted when the doctor entered with news that felt almost too good to be true: After extensive testing, there was no trace of the tumor or infection; the surgeon had gotten it all. The shift was staggering. Her body, once declared incurable, had responded beyond all expectations. It was a miracle. She shared the experience with her friend—how the voice had urged her to get up, how it promised the return of her daughter. Her friend listened in awe, uncertain what to say but deeply moved by Gaylynn's faith.

The words God had spoken to her in the ICU echoed in her mind, intertwining with the doctor's report. *"Get up. It's not your time."* They became her battle cry.

Despite the tubes, despite the marks, despite the permanent bag that now altered her daily life, Gaylynn's conviction was steadfast: God was not finished with her yet. This wasn't just about cancer. It was about resilience forged in suffering, courage birthed in fear, and faith that rises even in the darkest nights.

Though she could not yet see the full path ahead—one filled with both physical challenges and emotional restoration—Gaylynn embraced a single truth: She had to get up.

It was more than survival. It was defiance. A declaration of resilience. A testament to her relentless spirit. And in those fragile but determined steps forward, Gaylynn showed all of us that true courage is not the absence of fear but the will to rise despite it.

CHAPTER 18

A NEW ENEMY: FACING THE UNKNOWN

"Sometimes healing begins with the courage of others who refuse to let you go."— Author

After some time, Gaylynn was strong enough to be released from the hospital. Her friend and companion drove her back to his house where she would recuperate. The road to recovery, however, was anything but easy. Her body was gaunt, her skin pale, and her spirit dragged beneath the weight of loss. She was in pain most of the time, relying on a cocktail of high-level painkillers and medications prescribed after such an invasive surgery. But for a woman with a history of addiction, it was a dangerous combination.

I worried constantly about the ease with which the pills were prescribed. Doctors saw only her frail body and the severity of her surgery, not the history that lingered beneath the surface. To them, she was a patient in pain. To me, she was a survivor standing on a fault line, one wrong step away from unraveling.

The house itself was not the best environment for her recovery. Gaylynn struggled to keep food down, and she was still learning to navigate life with a colostomy bag. A nurse visited occasionally, teaching her how to care for the wound, change the bag, and adjust her diet, but progress was slow. Left alone for long stretches, Gaylynn slipped deeper into despair. She admitted that in those days she often wished for death to come quickly. She swallowed the pain medications throughout the day, not only to ease her suffering but to sleep—hoping unconsciousness would numb both her body and her heart.

Weeks turned into months, and her will to live dimmed. She knew she was desperately sick, but her longing to be reunited with her daughter was stronger than any desire to fight for her own life. Depression wrapped itself tightly around her, and denial became her only coping mechanism.

Her companion tried to help, but his efforts were inconsistent. He was patient at times, but often gone for hours, leaving her alone in a body that no longer felt like her own. As her health continued to fail, Gaylynn's reliance on him grew, though he was unable—or unwilling—to provide the support she truly needed. Gratitude and disappointment coexisted uneasily between them. She appreciated his presence yet began to sense how fragile their connection had become.

At one point, my daughter went to check on Gaylynn for me. Alarmed, she called immediately. She described what she saw with grave concern in her voice: Gaylynn was shockingly thin, her skin a grayish hue, lying weakly on the couch. When Gaylynn asked for her pain medication, my daughter opened the bedside drawer and froze. Everything had been dumped into the bottom of the drawer, pills jumbled together, stripped of order or labels. The smell of stale medicine and sickness clung to the room.

My daughter's voice cracked as she described the scene. She had grown up seeing Gaylynn as strong, vibrant, unbreakable. To witness her diminished to that state—thin, gray, surrounded by a tangle of pills—was almost more than she could bear. In her voice I heard both fear and sorrow, and I knew how deeply it shook her to see Gaylynn like that.

When I confronted Gaylynn later, she was defensive. She insisted she had accidentally spilled them while opening bottles and assured me she could tell which was which. I wasn't convinced. Over the phone, her words were sometimes jumbled, her voice distant. Still, when I went to see her myself, she appeared better than I expected—thin, yes, but coherent. I pressed her to come stay with me. She refused, offering excuses. Later, she admitted the truth: She didn't want to be a burden.

The weeks passed, and it became clear she would not survive much longer in that setting. I had been in constant contact with her younger sister, and together we decided something had to change. Despite their strained relationship, her sister went to see her. What she found stunned her: Gaylynn, asleep in bed, lying in her own filth, her body weakened, her skin sallow. Without hesitation, she cleaned her up, dressed her, and drove her straight to the doctor.

The physician's assessment was blunt: Gaylynn was on the verge of an unintentional overdose. The combination of painkillers, malnutrition, and weakness had left her teetering on the edge of death. This time, it was her younger sister who stepped in as rescuer, forcing the intervention that Gaylynn herself could not initiate.

For years, their relationship had been marked by silence, distance, and unspoken hurt. Gaylynn later admitted she barely remembered that day. But I doubt her sister would ever forget it—the smell of sickness, the frailty of the body she once clung to for protection as a child, the sharp realization that time was running out. In some ways, it was a reversal of roles: The younger sister, once shielded, now became the shield. But in that moment, none of it mattered. Gaylynn's younger sister moved with the determination of someone who refused to lose her again. It was as if the bond they had once clung to in childhood resurfaced, fierce and protective, cutting through the bitterness of the years between.

Gaylynn was readmitted to the hospital to stabilize her system and regain her stamina. And while her body remained frail, a spark of determination ignited that hadn't been there for a long time. Between her sister's intervention, the constant prayers from those who loved her, and the steady encouragement of a close friend who had also battled cancer, Gaylynn began to believe she might still have something left to fight for.

That friend, though living out of state, called her daily. Having walked her own road through cancer, she offered practical advice: what foods to juice, what nutrients to focus on, how to use diet as part of the healing process. She reminded Gaylynn that attitude mattered too, that despair could undo even the strongest treatment. Gaylynn credits much of her eventual recovery to this woman's guidance and to the way she refused to let her give up.

Slowly, Gaylynn began to turn a corner. Her appetite crept back, she gained a little stamina, and she became more mindful about what she put into her body. Still painfully thin and fragile, she was nevertheless finding her way back toward life. Each improvement was measured in the smallest of steps—an extra sip of juice, a short walk to the kitchen, a smile that lingered for more than a moment. Watching her make those halting steps forward stirred something in me too. It reminded me that even the smallest victories can echo louder than despair. To an outsider, it may have looked like nothing. To me, it was monumental. Each act of resilience, however slight, felt like a declaration that she was not finished.

And it was here, in her weakness, that I remembered the words of Isaiah: "He gives strength to the weary and increases the power of the weak" (40:29). That verse became my prayer over her daily. She had nothing left in herself, but I believed God was carrying her in ways none of us could.

But just as she began to recover, another tragedy unfolded. Her half sister—the same one whose addiction had long strained their relationship—was involved in a horrific accident. In many ways, her choices mirrored Gaylynn's own past struggles. One late night, while she was intoxicated and behind the wheel with her two young children in the car, she struck and killed a pedestrian. The news was a cruel reminder of the relentless cycle of destruction that had long defined their family's story.

The call came in the middle of the night. Gaylynn's mother's panic-stricken voice bled through the line, with children crying so loudly in the background that her words fractured with panic. Behind it all came her half sister's incoherent pleas. For a long moment, Gaylynn sat with the phone pressed against her ear, unable to breathe. It was as though the past had come roaring back, decades of family dysfunction distilled into one night of tragedy.

Without thinking, she dressed quickly, prepared to rush out the door to help. But on the way, she phoned one of her other siblings from her birth father's side. The words stopped her cold: "This is not your burden to carry. Turn around. Stop bailing her out."

Gaylynn's hands were shaking as she gripped the steering wheel, but she listened. She turned the car around. She drove in stillness, the ache of the decision bearing down harder than the steering wheel beneath her hands. Every mile felt like a tearing away—of habit, of history, of the instinct to rush in and fix what could not be fixed. Tears blurred the road, but beneath them was a surprising clarity: She could not save her half sister. She could only save herself.

The decision tore at her. She was angry at her half sister for endangering her own children and devastated for the pedestrian's family. But beneath the anger was sorrow—because she understood too well the grip of addiction, the destructive patterns it breeds, and the way it repeats itself generation after generation. In her half sister's actions, Gaylynn saw echoes of her own past, the patterns she had once lived and barely survived.

That moment in the car was a crossroads. Gaylynn could have followed the script—rushing in, taking responsibility, carrying a burden that was never hers. Instead, she turned back. Tears blurred her vision as she drove home, knowing she had chosen a different path. It was one of the hardest decisions of her life, but also one of the most freeing.

The tragedy left Gaylynn shaken, but it also clarified something for her: She could not carry the load of everyone else's brokenness.

She had to focus on her own body, mind, and spirit. That night, as she lay in bed, she prayed not for her sister, but for herself—a new and unsettling focus. It felt selfish, but it was necessary. She asked God for the resolve to break free from the patterns that had bound her family for so long, chains she had carried but refused to pass on. For the first time in a long while, her prayers were not only about survival, but about transformation.

Faced with this new heartache, Gaylynn once again turned inward, seeking solace in her faith and the path of self-preservation she had been trying to navigate. She began to understand that while she could not change others or control the turmoil around her, she could find what she needed within herself and her connection with God. Her recovery would not be simple or clearly defined; it would be a continuous quest of ups and downs, and one that she would ultimately have to walk alone—just her and God.

There would be setbacks, depression, and days when she wanted to withdraw. Much of that tendency went back to her childhood, when being sick meant being quiet, sent to bed in the dark so as not to disturb her stepfather. That learned silence had followed her into adulthood, making her reluctant to ask for help, determined not to inconvenience anyone. But slowly, she began to see that isolation would not save her this time.

In the end, what brought her back was not one person or one moment, but the convergence of many: her younger sister's intervention, her friend's persistent encouragement, the daily prayers of family, and the presence of God pressing in through it all.

Gaylynn was still fragile, still fighting, but she was alive. And more than that, she was choosing, however slowly, to keep moving forward, one small step at a time. In the months that followed, her relationship with her companion came to a quiet end. They parted ways and Gaylynn carried no bitterness—only gratitude for the man who had tried, in his own imperfect way, to walk beside her through the hardest stretch of her healing.

CHAPTER 19

THE RETURN OF LIGHT: A DAUGHTER'S HOMECOMING

"Think beautiful thoughts."
— *Gaylynn's daughter*

For nearly two years, Gaylynn had lived with the unrelenting silence of her daughter's absence. She once promised me she would not leave our hometown until her daughter was found, and she held to that vow with a stubbornness born of both grief and faith. Always in her mind was the promise she had heard while on life support, that her daughter would be found and returned on July 4. Every day of recovery, every small step forward was shadowed by that absence. Even as her body slowly healed, her heart remained tethered to waiting . . . for what only God could reveal.

News of the discovery didn't reach Gaylynn right away. For her, it began innocently enough—a phone call from a friend. She wouldn't learn the full account until later, but that call cracked open emotions she had tried so hard to keep shielded. As her friend spoke, the pieces of the puzzle fell into place, and Gaylynn found herself closer to the truth than she had been since that fateful weekend so long ago. The moment felt surreal—like being pulled out of one reality and thrust into another. Her breath caught as the details sank in. With a mixture of disbelief and relief, she realized her daughter was not lost forever.

Her fate, though painful, was finally revealed. Gaylynn's heart could finally begin to heal.

The answer came through the quiet faithfulness of a stranger. A local firefighter, a man Gaylynn had never met, often returned to the river where the accident had happened. Each time he went out on the water, he thought of Gaylynn's daughter and prayed for her return. Nearly two years passed, and still he remembered.

One afternoon, about a year after the accident, he was on the river with his sons when he noticed a wreath floating downstream. White and yellow blooms, battered by time, still clung to it. He pulled it from the water, cleaned it, and set it back afloat as a small act of reverence—a way of saying she was not forgotten.

Months later, in early July, he was back on the river. Before he even left shore, he noticed something unusual—a wooden beaded necklace with a small cross glinting in the sunlight. He picked it up, wiped it clean, and prayed for protection. Something about that moment stirred him. He couldn't shake the sense that this day would be different. He tucked the cross aside, promising himself he would come back for it when the day was done.

Hours later, as he and his sons rode along the familiar shoreline, his eyes caught what looked like a buoy. But as he drew closer, a terrible recognition settled in. He quickly steered his boys to a sandbar, instructing them to wait while he went back alone. The truth became undeniable: After nearly two years, Gaylynn's daughter had been found.

He stayed with her, unwilling to leave her side, even as the sun dropped lower in the sky. His instinct was to protect her, even then, to make sure she was not alone again. At last, he flagged down a passing boat and borrowed their phone to call the authorities. Once help arrived, he guided his children to safety, but before leaving, he returned to retrieve the wooden cross. Holding it in his hand, he gave thanks to God for guiding him that day, for protecting his sons, and for answering the prayer so many had prayed: Gaylynn's daughter was finally going home.

The coroner's office later confirmed what many called nothing short of a miracle. After nearly two years in the water, her body was completely intact. It was as though God Himself had preserved her for that moment.

Two days later, on July 4, Gaylynn's daughter was finally returned home—exactly as God had promised her when she lay in that hospital bed, fighting for her life. I remember Gaylynn telling me through tears, "He told me she would be brought home. And now, she is." In that moment, the long waiting gave way to the strange mixture of sorrow and relief that only faith can hold.

Closure does not erase the raw pain of losing a child, but it can soften its edges. Knowing her daughter had been found brought a release she hadn't dared to imagine. The ache remained, and always would, but the silence was over. She could finally carry her loss with certainty instead of questions. And in that certainty, a new strength began to rise—the return of light after a long, dark night.

Left behind, but never forgotten.

The world quieted the day she came home.

CHAPTER 20

THE COURAGE TO HEAL

"Dear friend, I pray that you may enjoy good health and that all may go well with you, even as your soul is getting along well."— *3 John 1:2*

While Gaylynn's struggle through cancer treatment had been long and grueling, her path forward began to transform. The focus was no longer only on what medicine could do to save her life, but on what she could do to nourish it. She began exploring a more holistic way of restoration, one that linked her body, mind, and spirit together. In many ways, this was not an entirely new journey, for she had already begun making small changes before her diagnosis. But it wasn't until she attended a yoga retreat in Mexico, just before the cancer revealed itself, that she began to truly grasp the connection between what she consumed and how she lived.

A few days into the retreat, Gaylynn strolled into class holding a meat lover's pizza, the aroma of grease and cheese rising from the box, grease pooling at the corners of the cardboard. The instructor, smiling with gentle humor, pointed at the pizza and said, "Oh, that will change!" Gaylynn, never one to back down from a moment of banter, quipped back, "I'm hungry, and you're working us to death!" The room laughed. For Gaylynn, humor had always been a shield, a way to keep things light, to mask discomfort. She continued her old eating pattern as the retreat continued.

But by the fourth day, the joke no longer landed. While the other participants glowed with energy, she was sluggish, her limbs leaden, her body refusing to cooperate. She sat cross-legged on her mat, her breath ragged against the steady rhythm of others moving with ease. It was then she realized something she had long resisted: What she put into her body mattered. Food wasn't just fuel; it was either supporting her or sabotaging her. That realization wasn't subtle; it hit her with the same force as the fatigue in her limbs. She told me later how she sat on her mat, watching the others move with ease, their bodies light and unburdened. Meanwhile, hers felt slow, as though dragged down by years of choices she had dismissed as harmless. The contrast was undeniable, and in that moment, the pizza she had carried in so proudly seemed almost symbolic of the old patterns she knew she would have to let go.

That moment marked a turning point, a lesson that would later become a cornerstone of her recovery.

As Gaylynn's body slowly regained endurance after the darkest stretch of her treatment, she carried with her another ache—the mourning of her daughter's death. Physical mending was measured in pounds gained, steps walked, foods tolerated. But her heart carried an invisible wound that could not be stitched or sutured. Every green juice, every yoga pose held longer than the day before, every small victory in her recovery reminded her that her daughter was not there to see it.

She began building her days around small rituals of care. In the early mornings, she could be found on her mat, stretching through the pain, reclaiming space in a body she once felt betrayed by. Then she would juice vegetables and sip slowly, as though each swallow was an act of gratitude. Long morning walks with her beloved dog, Sunny, followed shortly after. At night, she settled into bed with a cup of freshly made ginger tea, closing her eyes in prayer and offering thanks for making it through another day.

Sometimes the longing for her daughter surfaced in sharp, unexpected ways. She would reach for her phone after a good day of treatment, ready to call and share the progress—only to remember she wasn't there to answer. The emptiness on the other end became its own kind of wound. Even in moments of triumph, heartache pulled her back, reminding her that no amount of healthy food or stronger muscles could fill the absence at her table. Her sadness surfaced in places she couldn't predict—sometimes in the middle of a yoga pose, sometimes at the quiet end of the day when her body was exhausted but her mind refused to rest.

Some days the sadness threatened to undo the progress her body was making. At times, she slipped back into depression, overwhelmed by the realization that her body could not erase the ache of loss . . . especially on her daughter's birthday or the anniversary of her death.

Yet slowly, Gaylynn began to see that her loss, though permanent, did not have to define her. Her repairing was not only physical but layered with emotional and spiritual work. She began to confront wounds she had carried for years: childhood trauma, fractured family relationships, and the pain that still hung over her like a veil. Her healthier lifestyle choices became a mirror of that deeper work. As she cleansed her body internally, she was also tending to the broken places of her soul.

For the first time, Gaylynn began to see that her survival was not solely about cancer. It was about learning how to live again—even with pain as a companion.

During this season, her spiritual life began to deepen in ways she hadn't expected. She told me she could sense God's presence more clearly than ever before. One memory in particular anchored her: the afternoon she danced with her daughter on the beach, just a day before tragedy struck. That moment became a gift she carried with her—a reassurance that love endured beyond what the eyes could see. It was a touchstone for her, proof that God was real and that He was holding both her and her daughter. When she shared the story with others, she often said with a confident and bold conviction,

"I know God is real; He gave me one last dance on the beach with my daughter."

Prayer, once distant, became daily bread. In moments of despair, when she was too weak to move, she would offer a simple prayer for energy, sometimes in words, sometimes only in groans. And in those moments, she said, God spoke back—not with thunder, but with a quiet assurance that she was not alone.

From the outside, her changes might have seemed small, but to me they were monumental. I found myself watching for them each time we spoke: Was her voice steadier, her laugh more ready, her step a little stronger? Even in her weakness, I prayed over her daily, asking God to magnify every small gain into a promise of more to come. She began setting healthy boundaries, especially with men, no longer seeking worth through relationships that drained her. It wasn't dramatic at first, more like quiet decisions made one after another. She stopped answering calls from people who only reached out when they needed something. She declined invitations that once would have pulled her into unhealthy patterns. For the first time in a long time, she wasn't afraid to say no. In those choices, I saw internal growth happening within her; she was beginning to value herself, not for what she gave to others, but for who she was becoming. She grew more mindful of how she treated her body, seeing nutrition and care not as punishment but as a way of honoring the life God had spared.

It struck me that what was happening to Gaylynn wasn't just recovery. It was restoration.

Through prayer and reflection, she began to see that God had been present all along, even in her deepest valleys. The pain of her daughter's loss would always remain, but she began to frame it differently—not as an ending, but as part of a story in which grace was still at work.

Rehabilitation rarely moved in a straight line; it bent and wavered, sometimes circling back before moving forward again. There were days of progress, and there were days of exhaustion.

But the more she nourished her body, the more she felt her spirit developing a resolve. Each meal prepared with care, each boundary honored, each prayer whispered in faith became an act of defiance against despair.

In time, Gaylynn came to believe that her restoration—physical, emotional, and spiritual—was part of God's plan for her life. Survival had once been her only goal. Now she began to see something more: a life not only endured but embraced. Her journey was guiding her toward purpose, toward understanding, toward a relationship with God that went deeper than anything she had known before.

She was still fragile, still marked by wounds visible and unseen. But she was also stronger, steadier, and more whole than she had been in years. The one who had once walked into yoga class with a pizza in hand was becoming a woman who recognized the sacredness of caring for her body and her soul.

And perhaps that was the truest sign for her: Gaylynn was no longer living only to survive; she was learning, at last, to thrive.

What struck me most was not only the progress of her body, but the quiet transformation of her spirit. Renewal rarely announces itself with trumpets; it creeps in slowly, through choices made in silence when no one is listening. Gaylynn's journey in those days reminded me that survival is a gift, but learning to live again is a calling. Her wounds remained, her mourning was still present, but beneath it all, something new was taking root: personal grit that no sickness could erase and a spirit that no loss could extinguish.

CHAPTER 21

HELGA'S ROAR

"She is clothed with strength and dignity; she can laugh at the days to come."— *Proverbs 31:25*

The burden of everything Gaylynn had endured began to shift as she took steps toward rebuilding her life. The heartache of losing her daughter, the brutal battle with cancer, the reminders that had marked her body and her spirit—were still a part of her story, but they no longer held her captive. Each new day brought with it a more consistent connection to God, guiding her toward a new purpose: helping others who were lost in their own darkness. The pain would never disappear, but she was no longer constrained by it. Instead, she found her grit in survival, and that fortitude became the light she carried with her—ready to share with the world.

True to her nature, Gaylynn refused to remain still. She was no longer bound by her promise to never leave her hometown; with her daughter finally home, Gaylynn could go anywhere with a clear conscience. She often said, "If I've got fifty bucks in my pocket and my passport, I can travel anywhere." For her, change was not a threat but a form of oxygen. So, when the idea of moving to Florida arose, it felt less like an escape and more like a continuation of her lifelong rhythm: seeking new horizons.

Her dear friend—the one who had called her daily through the darkest stretch of chemo—was also looking for a fresh start. After many conversations, the two decided to make the leap together. Gaylynn borrowed $5,000 from me, packed her car with a few belongings, her sweet dog, and the resilience that had carried her this far. She was determined to make Florida her new beginning.

But Gaylynn couldn't leave without extending an invitation to her half sister. After more than twenty years of abuse, her sister had finally left her ruthless husband. She was fragile, trying to stay sober, and had lost custody of her children after the tragic accident she caused while intoxicated. Gaylynn, always quick to forgive, wanted to offer her a chance at redemption. She invited her to come along on the road trip—company for Gaylynn on the long drive, and a fresh start for her half sister.

The trip across the country was anything but easy. Because money was tight, they stayed in cheap motels, the kind with stale air, flickering lights, and locks that barely worked. Gaylynn called me every day, her voice steady but edged with fatigue, updating me on the road ahead. But it soon became clear her half sister's addictions were deeper than she realized. Withdrawal hit hard, pulling her into terrifying spirals of sickness and agitation. One night, Gaylynn woke to find her sister missing. Panic rushed in as she threw on her shoes and ran into the night. She found her in the parking lot, sitting in a car with a stranger, using drugs under the cover of darkness. Gaylynn's heart broke at the sight. She didn't yell or berate her. She simply pulled her away, got back to their room, and packed up. By morning, they were back on the road.

The miles stretched long between them. Sometimes her sister muttered apologies, other times she stayed on her phone playing games, or she sat stone silent, staring out the window as if the world outside held answers she couldn't find inside herself. Gaylynn gripped the wheel, torn between anger and compassion. She wanted to scream at her for squandering another chance, but instead she drove in silence, praying under her breath that this time would be different. Every passing exit sign felt like a measure of both distance and disappointment—moving closer to Florida, but not closer to the sister she was trying to rescue.

At last, they arrived in Florida. For a few days, there was a fragile sense of calm. Gaylynn's half sister seemed steadier, the color returning faintly to her face. But the reprieve was short-lived. She asked to borrow the golf cart Gaylynn and her friend had rented, promising to be back quickly. Hours later she returned, and scattered across the cart were miniature liquor bottles. The relapse was undeniable.

That was the last straw. With an aching heart, Gaylynn put her half sister on a plane and sent her home. It was one of the hardest decisions she had ever made. She knew all too well the sting of tough love; she had been on the receiving end many times herself. To now be the one forced to draw the line left her shaken, but she also knew it was necessary. She could not sacrifice her own fragile recovery to rescue someone unwilling to be helped.

For Gaylynn, Florida marked a turning point. Beyond distance from family disarray, it was space to begin living again. Yet even here, life wasn't simple. She carried into Florida the reality of her cancer treatments and the daily presence of her colostomy bag.

Gaylynn never lost her sense of humor, though, and humor soon became one of her most powerful survival tools. In the early months after surgery, she realized how unpredictable the bag could be—gurgling and roaring at the most inconvenient moments. Despite the erratic uncertainty of having it, she decided if it was going to be with her permanently, it needed a name. With a mischievous grin, she christened it "Helga." "If she's going to roar, she might as well have a name," Gaylynn said.

Helga's "roars" became part of Gaylynn's story. She told them with such candor that they often ended in laughter, though the reality wasn't always funny in the moment. Once, at the grocery store deli counter, Helga let out a loud, unmistakable sound. A man turned and snapped, "Well, excuse YOU!" Mortified, her cheeks burned as she darted through the aisles until she found her friend, blurting out what happened. Her friend laughed until tears rolled down her cheeks, later saying she'd never seen Gaylynn run so fast.

On another occasion, while standing in line at a store, Helga made herself known again. The woman beside her rolled her eyes with disgust. Without hesitation, Gaylynn lifted her shirt just enough to reveal the colostomy bag. The woman's face went pale. Without a word, she walked away, shame replacing judgment. Gaylynn would later joke that Helga had a bigger personality than most people she knew. "She's got no filter—just like me—and absolutely no respect for timing." Friends began to ask her, half serious, "How's Helga today?" It became part of her daily storytelling, a way to turn embarrassment into amusement. Humor gave her power back; it was better to laugh first than to let anyone else laugh at her.

These moments were Gaylynn in her truest form: refusing to let shame steal her joy.

Still, some days living with Helga were anything but funny. The odors were a constant battle, and supplies came at a steep cost. Without insurance, Gaylynn had to stretch every dollar and grow creative in her approach. She figured out which brands held up best in water, which bags could be patched, and how to clean and reuse one when money ran short. Each adjustment demanded determination, resourcefulness, and grit—qualities Gaylynn had in abundance.

Sometimes the challenges caught her off guard. While visiting me one autumn, we went together to watch my grandson's football game. Partway through, she leaned over and quietly said that she wasn't feeling well and wanted to go back to my house. Trying to lighten the mood, I joked, "Maybe Helga needs checking." The smell near us had been sharp and unpleasant; however, she claimed she didn't smell anything. Later that night, she called to say her Uber driver had rolled down all the windows for the ride home—even in the crisp fall evening. The next morning, she tested positive for COVID. She laughed about it, shaking her head. "Of course God would give me COVID and take away my sense of smell. Proof He has a sense of humor."

Through it all, Gaylynn refused to be limited. With Helga in tow, she swam, took surf lessons, even went scuba diving again. On the beach, she was herself: joyful, bold, unafraid of darting looks or pointing fingers. Each awkward outing was matched by a moment where she reclaimed her life, inch by inch, with what she carried.

However, during her time with Helga, Gaylynn faced countless obstacles, each one forcing her to adapt to a radically different way of life. The transition wasn't easy; adjusting to the physical realities of living with a colostomy bag was a constant struggle. While she learned to manage the sounds, the odor remained an ever-present challenge, one that she had to contend with daily. Yet, Gaylynn found ways to navigate public outings, carefully timing them to minimize both the sounds and the smells. She even mastered the delicate art of managing her own care, learning how to tend to the wound with precision. Her ability to find practical solutions, no matter the difficulty, was a testament to her resilience and perseverance.

After some time, she found herself in a relationship with a new man who became a significant part of her life. He was kind, patient, and accepting, especially as she navigated intimacy with Helga. Yet, despite his compassion, his lack of support during her more challenging moments revealed a stark contrast. It was an important relationship, but it ultimately wasn't the right one for her.

Then came the scare that threatened to undo it all.

After building a new rhythm in Florida, she began to feel unwell again. Her dear friend drove her to the hospital, where scans showed what appeared to be a mass on her liver. The ER doctor spoke bluntly: The cancer had likely returned. He urged her to see an oncologist immediately. The news shook her to the core. After everything, was she about to face the same nightmare again?

But Gaylynn, in her typical way, refused to let fear choose her next step. Before she saw the specialist, she bought a ticket to Cuba and the Bahamas. "If I'm leaving this world," she said to a friend, "let my goodbye be in the water, diving." In the days afterward she oscillated between boldness and a low foreboding. She packed her backpack with what looked like courage but felt like desperation;

every item became a small practice in farewell. She told me she prayed in a new way then—not pleading for repair, but asking God that if it was her time, she might go doing what set her alive. Under the bravado, the question remained: Could she handle another round of suffering?

She swam the turquoise sea, salt crusting her skin, laughter on the surface and a quiet unease beneath. Those days were full and free: Beauty lived alongside the unknown.

However, God was not done writing her story.

When she returned from what she thought was her last jaunt in the ocean, she met with the surgeon. He studied her scans, ran further tests, and then surprised her with words she hadn't dared believe: There was no tumor. The mass was scar tissue from previous surgeries. And then came the shock that left her reeling: He believed it was time to consider reversal surgery. Helga, her literal sidekick, might be removed.

Gaylynn broke down in tears. For five years, she had lived with Helga. She had accepted her as permanent, even grown to fold her into her sense of humor and resilience. To imagine life without her was overwhelming. Could she dare to dream that her body might be restored in such a profound way? For years, Helga had been her constant companion—loud, inconvenient, but also proof she had survived. To consider life without her felt almost like betrayal, as if removing Helga would erase the evidence of what she had fought through. And yet, optimism stirred. She thought of swimming again without hesitation of what others might think, of sitting in a quiet room without sudden roars, of feeling whole in a way she hadn't in years. The thought was almost too much to grasp.

Watching her tears slip down her trembling face, the surgeon prayed with her that day, holding her hands as he encouraged her to choose to believe. Slowly, she nodded. The decision was made.

It would not be easy. Reversal surgery carried its own risks, and the road to recovery would be long. But Gaylynn faced it with the same grit she had brought to every battle before. Florida had become a place of survival, of laughter, of heartbreak, and now, of possibility. And as she prepared for the next chapter, she carried with her the voice of resilience that had never left:

Helga might have roared, but Gaylynn roared louder.

I often think of this season as proof that survival is rarely neat. Gaylynn's life in Florida was messy, unpredictable, at times heartbreaking—and yet, it was also marked by laughter, grit, and a stubborn insistence on optimism. Watching her adapt, even to something as intrusive as a colostomy bag, reminded me that resilience isn't about waiting for life to return to what it was. It's about finding courage in what remains, and even more, in what can still be reclaimed.

CHAPTER 22

A NEW BEGINNING: LIFE AFTER HELGA

"Strength grows in the moments when you think you can't go on but you keep going anyway."— *Unknown*

Even with the reassurance of her compassionate surgeon, Gaylynn wavered. The decision to undergo reversal surgery—the chance to live without Helga—was both a dream and a terror. For years she had accepted the bag as permanent, telling its "roaring" stories with a mix of her signature humor, candor, and grit. Now she faced the possibility of life without it, and the thought unsettled her as much as it thrilled her.

In the weeks leading up to the surgery, her emotions ran raw. She researched recovery stories late into the night, scrolling through accounts that painted the path as long, painful, and uncertain. Her imagination often outpaced reality, convincing her that she wouldn't make it through. Fear set in, and she called often, crying into the phone. "I just feel so alone," she admitted, her voice thin with exhaustion. I wanted to be with her, to hold her hand, to comfort her, but circumstances kept me away. Thankfully, her dear friend that had moved to Florida with her stayed by her side. Together we prayed, believing that the same God who had carried her through the darkest nights would not abandon her now.

Part of Gaylynn's loneliness, I would later learn, came from the silence of the man she had been seeing. Despite his earlier affection, he never once showed up at the hospital or offered support during her recovery. His absence cut deep, a reminder of the fractured relationships that had so often shaped her life. She kept glancing at the doorway, half hoping he might appear, but it stayed empty. What wounded her most was not the pain of surgery but the quiet from those she expected to be there. She had weathered abandonment before—from broken marriages, from fractured family ties—but this time, in her most vulnerable state, it cut deeper. "It's when you're flat on your back that you find out who really loves you," she said to me once. And in that season, the list was shorter than she ever imagined. In contrast, her surgeon was steady, explaining each step, walking her through the risks with patience and compassion. Before she went under anesthesia, she gave him my contact information, wanting me to be the first to know if things turned dire.

The surgery was expected to last an hour and a half. Instead, it stretched to nine and a half grueling hours. Scar tissue from previous operations, years of living with Helga, and the fragile condition of her intestines turned what should have been routine into a test of persistence. The surgeon later told me there were moments he nearly stopped. Her body was fragile, scar tissue dense, and every move carried risk. Yet in those moments, he prayed. "I asked God for steady hands," he told me. "And each time, I felt a quiet resolve to continue." His persistence mirrored Gaylynn's own—both refusing to give up even when the odds whispered otherwise. By the time he emerged to call me, his voice echoed the strain, and the exhaustion and reverence was loud and clear. "By the grace of God, we were able to finish the surgery," he said.

Gaylynn woke to find herself alive, but the hard part was just beginning. The surgeon explained that her recovery would take seven to ten days in the hospital, long enough for her body to relearn how to function without the colostomy. She needed to rest, to let restoration happen slowly, to accept the care being offered. But Gaylynn had never been one for slow.

After only five days, she insisted on leaving. Gaylynn hated hospitals. To her, they weren't places of mending but places of loss, memories of loved ones who never walked out. She would rather risk her own health than feel trapped within those walls another day. Stubbornness carried her out the doors, but it was a decision that nearly cost her everything. Despite warnings, she checked herself out, assuring everyone that she'd be fine. Her dear friend picked her up and promised me she would monitor her medications and keep her safe. I wanted to believe it, but a pit in my stomach told me Gaylynn's stubbornness might soon outrun her recovery.

Back at home, the pain proved relentless. Her body, fragile from surgery, protested every move. Nights were the worst—long stretches where she tossed and turned, unable to sleep. Desperate for relief, she persuaded her friend to give her control of her own medication. It was a dangerous bargain. As a recovering addict, Gaylynn's relationship with pills had always been fraught, and now, mixed with legitimate pain, the risk grew sharper.

When I spoke with her during those days, her voice was often slurred, her words jumbled. I knew she was hurting, but the full picture was hidden from me. I prayed harder, asking God to steady her, to protect her from her own impulses.

Her new roommate was the one who finally sounded the alarm. Though quiet and reserved, she noticed the signs—Gaylynn doubled over in the bathroom, her body too weak to stand, vomiting until pain etched across her face. The roommate called Gaylynn's friend, who rushed her back to the hospital.

There, doctors discovered a severe intestinal blockage. "It's a miracle she's even walking," one said. The blockage had twisted her insides into knots of agony, leaving her body unable to function. She was readmitted immediately, this time for seventeen long days.

Those seventeen days felt like a wilderness. No food, no control, nothing to cling to except God. "I can't do this," she uttered more than once. Yet in that stripping away, she discovered what had always been true: Survival didn't depend on her striving but on surrender. Each IV drip, each labored breath became its own kind of prayer, a rhythm of dependence she had long resisted. She was restricted to a dry fast—nothing by mouth, not even water. Fluids came only through an IV. Her lips cracked with dryness, every breath rasping as she longed for water she could not drink. Desperate for even the smallest relief, she begged nurses for ice chips. One relented, placing a few in a cup. She promised not to swallow any, only to let them melt on her tongue. That small act—the coolness against her lips, the sensation of water she could not drink—was a reminder that even in deprivation, mercy could still appear.

When I called her during those days, her words pierced me. "I regret it," she confessed, "I should never have agreed to the reversal," her voice ragged with pain. "I want Helga back." For a woman who had once joked about her colostomy bag's antics, who had fought so hard to move forward, this change of heart showed how deep her suffering ran. She longed for the security of what she had already survived, even if it meant sacrificing belief for what might come.

And yet, even then, something stronger glimmered beneath the despair. Though she cried, though she doubted, though she wished at times to be released from it all, she never let go entirely. Somewhere in the stillness of those nights, Gaylynn held on.

The seventeen days passed slowly, a grind of medical routines, halting prayers, and a body learning again to cooperate. Each day the nurses marveled at her tenacity. Each day, her friend would call or simply show up, refusing to let her sink into isolation.

Eventually, Gaylynn turned a corner. She was frail—gaunt and weak, her body still unsteady—but she was alive. And more than that, she was determined. "If I made it through that," she said later, "I can make it through anything."

Her story in those days was one of medical resilience but also a testament to her character—the stubborn refusal to quit, the defiance of despair, the way she clawed her way back even when she had nothing left. The doctor called it a miracle of surgery. I saw it as a miracle of faith.

Gaylynn's recovery after that point was slow but steady. Each day she managed to eat a little more, walk a little farther, breathe a little deeper. And with every tentative gain, she began to imagine life not defined by pain, not limited by Helga but marked by possibility.

She had always believed her life carried a greater purpose, though at times it had been buried beneath shadows of the past. Now, in the wake of the reversal surgery, she began to see glimpses of it. Her stubbornness—the same force that nearly cost her life by checking out early and pushing too hard—was also the force that propelled her forward. It was the very grit that would one day allow her to speak into the lives of others who had been broken, addicted, grieving.

This was not simply a new chapter for Gaylynn. It was a foreshadowing of the greater mission that awaited her: to stand in front of others and say, "I've been there. I've wanted to quit. But there is life beyond the pain."

The road was still long, and setbacks still came, but in those seventeen days of fasting, of pain, of unspoken regrets and fragile prayers, Gaylynn discovered something no surgeon could stitch and no medication could supply: She was still here for a reason.

I see now that those weeks became a kind of training ground. In the furnace of pain, Gaylynn learned what it meant to endure when endurance itself seemed impossible. She didn't know then that one day she would stand in front of others, sharing her story not as someone untouched by suffering but as someone who had lived through it. Her wounds were not signs of defeat; they were credentials for the mission ahead.

What she didn't know then was that the very etchings she carried would one day become her testimony.

She wore courage—even when it came with Velcro straps.

ACT V

HEALING

"But I will restore you to health and heal your wounds, declares the Lord." — Jeremiah 30:17

For years, the chapters of Gaylynn's life had been marked by loss and survival. A childhood shaped by brokenness, a family splintered by addiction, the sudden death of her daughter, and the shadow of a relentless disease; each chapter left damage that ran deep. Yet even the rough lines of healing told a story: not of defeat, but of endurance.

By the time she reached this season of her life, Gaylynn had endured battles that could have undone her. Her body bore the marks of surgeries, her heart carried the ache of loss, but neither was the measure of who she was. What carried her forward was the same strength that had sustained her through every trial: an unyielding resilience, fueled by faith, that refused to let despair be the finale.

This was never just about survival. It was about return—of hope, of joy, of promises long deferred. The morning was breaking, and Gaylynn was ready to step into its light.

CHAPTER 23

AGAINST THE ODDS: GAYLYNN'S JOURNEY BACK TO LIFE

"Out of difficulties grow miracles."
— *Jean de La Bruyère*

It took Gaylynn months to recover from the surgery to remove Helga. Her body had to adjust to the new normal—life with a smaller intestine and colon. Her doctor informed her that it could take up to two years for her to fully return to normal. During this period, Gaylynn committed herself to healthy living and eating. She dove deeper into researching the right foods and juices to support her health, considering her medical history. Never one to sit by and do nothing, she continued walking daily and practiced yoga regularly.

She had always equated rest with weakness, and so even in those delicate months she resisted slowing down. I remember her calling me after a long walk, her voice light but edged with fatigue. She laughed it off, as she so often did—"I just needed to stretch my legs"— but I could hear the pain she tried to hide. I reminded her of the doctor's orders, but Gaylynn had never been one to accept limits, even from her own body.

Yet her stubborn streak often pushed her further than her body could handle. Friends begged her to slow down, reminding her of the doctor's warnings, but Gaylynn brushed them off. "If I stop, I'll never start again," she told me. That determination had carried her through abuse and addiction, through losses of many kinds, but now it worked against her. She would push until she collapsed, then rest only long enough to rise and push again. Watching her, I sometimes wondered if she was trying to outrun the pain rather than heal from it.

As she settled into her new routine, Gaylynn developed close friendships and returned to enjoying the activities and beautiful scenery Florida had to offer: the bright bougainvillea, the heavy air scented faintly with rain, the wide skies and canopies of trees stretching above her walks. She felt great and had such a renewed sense of life most of the time, though she occasionally had hurdles—moments of not feeling well, or various aches and pains. As she often said, "Anyone who has survived cancer has a heightened awareness of their health. Every little ache or pain causes you to assume the cancer is back."

Gaylynn's favorite place to pray has always been on a beach or in a quiet, solitary spot. After everything she had endured, these moments became even more sacred to her. She longed for a deeper connection with God.

Through her new friendships, she found a small church and began attending regularly. She quickly connected with the people, enjoyed listening to the pastor, and felt very welcomed. The little church soon became more than a place of worship; it became a family. Members checked on her when she wasn't feeling well, prayed with her after services, and listened with patience when she shared pieces of her story. For someone who had felt so abandoned by people she trusted, this outpouring of acceptance gave her courage to keep showing up. She once laughed and said, "I finally found a family that doesn't run when things get messy."

Inspired by the newfound peace she was cultivating, Gaylynn, with the constant support of her dear friend, began teaching small groups at the church about health and wellness. These classes quickly gained traction, with people eager to hear her insights and share in her growth. True to her nature, Gaylynn brought a palpable energy and passion to each session, weaving her own story of renewal and transformation into the lessons she shared.

She approached each class with the same passion she carried into all her adventures. She brought jars of green juice for people to taste, demonstrated stretches that eased tension, and shared stories of both failure and triumph. More than once, participants left in tears, others nodding with murmurs of agreement as they heard their own struggles mirrored in her testimony. It wasn't polished or rehearsed; it was raw and real. And it was that realness that drew people in, convincing them that restoration wasn't for the lucky few but for anyone willing to keep trying.

After each class, people lingered long after the session ended, drawn not only to the information but to the authenticity in Gaylynn's voice. She had a way of making wellness feel less like a lecture and more like a conversation among friends. One woman said, "She doesn't just talk about it—she lives it, and you can feel it in the room."

It was clear to everyone around Gaylynn that she was changing; her presence, once defined by resilience, now radiated a warmth that could not be ignored. Gaylynn had always been unique, but in this new phase of her recovery, her light shone brighter than ever.

She spoke openly about her past struggles, hardships, and heartbreaks, but more powerfully, she shared the relentless pursuit of recovery—both physical and spiritual. During this time, Gaylynn and I kept in touch daily, with our conversations a safe space for her to share both her triumphs and her frustrations. At one point, she confided that she felt ready to pursue counseling—a decision I saw as a significant step in her mending. Together, we discussed the potential benefits of confronting the pain she'd carried for so long. Encouraged by our conversations, Gaylynn took the courageous step to seek therapy from the pastor at her church, who was also a licensed therapist.

Unfortunately, her time with therapy was short-lived. After only a few sessions, Gaylynn abruptly stopped attending. When I asked her why, she was hesitant to open up about it and quickly brushed off my questions. At first, I assumed it was because she wasn't quite ready to face the demons that had haunted her for so long. But the truth was far more painful. During her last session with the pastor, he made an inappropriate advance toward her; one that, tragically, was all too familiar to Gaylynn. She ended the session immediately, her stomach tightening as she walked out, fists balled at her sides in anger at the violation of trust again.

She had walked into those sessions with her signature shield—bravery, boldness, and humor—but on the inside, she truly wanted to begin to heal. For Gaylynn, trusting a man in a position of authority was no small step; her past had taught her to be wary. That's what made his betrayal cut even deeper. It wasn't just an inappropriate advance; it was the shattering of a tentative trust she had only recently begun to rebuild.

It could have been the breaking point—the moment she turned away from faith entirely. Instead, it became another place where her tenacity deepened.

For days afterward, she replayed the session in her mind, trying to make sense of it. She wondered if she had done something wrong, if she had misunderstood, but deep down, she knew the truth. The violation reopened reminders of earlier betrayals in her life, cutting into the tender place where trust was only beginning to grow again. "I should've known better," she uttered under her breath once, though I reminded her the blame was not hers to carry. Still, it took time for her to accept that truth.

Despite this wounding setback, Gaylynn refused to let it halt her progress. My concern for her, however, ran deep. Given her raw emotional state, particularly in regard to her relationship with God and her desire to deepen that connection, I feared that this experience might undo all the progress she had made. I worried that this betrayal, this violation of her trust, might cause her to retreat from the very faith that had been her rock.

In those days, she often texted or called asking me to get back on the Batphone. She said it half in jest, but I knew she was serious; she wanted the reassurance of someone holding her up in prayer when she felt too weak to do it herself. Each time, I reminded her gently, "You've got the same Batphone, Gaylynn; you just have to use it." Sometimes she'd brush it off with a laugh, but other times she'd go quiet, and I knew she was letting the reminder sink in.

Little by little, through her prayers scribbled in journals, she began picking up that line for herself. What started as borrowed energy became her own, one prayer at a time.

True to her spirit, Gaylynn persisted. She began journaling faithfully—using it as a tool to reflect, process, and regain a sense of self. With this renewed focus, she began to rebuild. Her journals began to fill not only with her private struggles but also with reflections she trusted might one day help others. She started jotting down phrases like "Pain doesn't get the last word" and "Rebuilding is stubborn work." They began as reminders to herself, scraps of courage scribbled in the margins. But as her notebook filled, it became clear she was preparing—perhaps unconsciously—to one day put those words into the hands of others who needed them.

As Gaylynn embraced the process of reflection and growth, her spiritual life became her greatest ally. With renewed purpose, she emerged stronger, more self-aware, and determined to continue living with intention. This new phase in her life was not without its challenges, but it was marked by a profound transformation—a transformation not only of body, but of heart and soul.

Her recovery was far from easy. She endured many hurdles along the way, days when old pain returned or when fatigue pulled her under like a tide. Yet there was also an unmistakable sense of direction, as though every trial was preparing her for something more. Slowly, her story wove itself into something larger, where cancer and loss intertwined with resilience rooted in the God who would not let go.

It was the beginning of something new: a mission that would lead her to share her hard-won wisdom with others who were ready to walk their own paths toward transformation. Recovering had not erased her wounds; it had given them meaning. And with that meaning came a quiet summons—to live beyond survival and offer a glimpse of mending to those still searching for their own way forward.

CHAPTER 24

LOOKING BACK TO MOVE FORWARD

"Do you not know that your bodies are temples of the Holy Spirit . . . Therefore honor God with your bodies."
— 1 Corinthians 6:19–20

Years earlier, in Belize, mornings often found her standing barefoot on the dock outside her small home. The water shimmered in the first light of dawn, pelicans gliding low, the air still cool from the night. The boards beneath her feet were rough, salt-worn, and damp with morning dew. Gulls cried overhead, their sharp calls carrying across the water, while the faint clink of a fisherman's net echoed from down the shore. The rhythm of waves against the pilings rose and fell like a hymn, mingling with the smell of seaweed drifting in on the tide. She would watch the sun rise slow and deliberate, streaking the horizon in pinks and oranges, and it felt to her like God's hand lifting the world awake. The sound of the waves and the hush of wind became her sanctuary. Out there, away from the noise and demands, she felt closest to her Creator. It was a sacred rhythm—one that steadied her in seasons when life threatened to spin out of control.

Prayer became her lifeline. It wasn't elaborate or refined but raw and simple, words spilling from a heart that had been broken more times than it should have. That weathered stretch of boards, with its salt-soaked air, became her church. The sea was her congregation. And each sunrise—slow, steady, insistent—reminded her that mercy really was new every morning.

Later, when she relocated to Florida, she carried that rhythm with her. Florida's beaches offered their own kind of sacred space. The warmth of the sand, the sweep of palm trees bending in the breeze, the steady roar of the Atlantic—all of it echoed what she had first discovered in Belize: that God often speaks loudest in the stillness of His creation.

But it wasn't until after Helga was gone—her colostomy bag that had been both a necessity and a burden—that Gaylynn felt a new door open. The removal marked more than a medical milestone; it was a release, a shedding of one more reminder of cancer's grip. She had survived the surgeries, endured the pain, and carried humiliations no one else could see. Afterward, following an encounter with a manipulative pastor and early mornings of reflection, she returned to the practice of journaling, this time with renewed purpose.

At first, the words came tentatively, written in uneven lines, as though she wasn't sure she was allowed to put them down. But soon the pages filled faster. Her journal became a confidant, a safe place where she could name the pain and still record gratitude. On those pages she poured out her fears, her dreams, her stubborn faith. She wrestled with God in ink and confession, wrote prayers for her daughters, and sometimes only scribbled single words: help, forgive, breathe.

That act of writing was not small. It was a turning point. For a woman who had once been silenced by abuse and hardship, who had swallowed her pain to survive, journaling became a voice reclaimed. The scratch of pen against paper, ink smudging her fingers where tears had fallen, became part of her story. She often wrote early in the morning, the room lit only by a single lamp, pages filling as the world outside fell silent. In those hours, the paper seemed to listen better than people ever could. Each entry's significance went beyond words—it was proof she had survived another day. Each page was a release, and at the same time, a record: of wounds endured, of faith tested, of grace uncovered.

Living in Florida offered her a new pace, one far different from the turbulence of the past. Sunshine stretched wide over her days. Palm fronds swayed overhead. The air smelled faintly of salt and blooming hibiscus, and every evening the sky put on a show as though God Himself painted it just for her. The humid air clung lightly to her skin, warm but oddly comforting. Florida gave her more than scenery; it mirrored the peace she was slowly cultivating inside, with the sound of distant lawnmowers humming and doves cooing in the late afternoons. It was beauty she never took for granted, because she had lived without it for so long.

The peace of Florida became the backdrop, but her true richness was measured in how she lived toward others.

Through it all, Gaylynn's generous heart remained unchanged. She had always been the one to give, even when she had little to spare. Her generosity wasn't showy or calculated; it was woven into who she was. If she had a dollar, she would share it. If she had a meal, someone else would eat too.

One memory still rises sharp in my mind from a visit I made to Florida. We were sitting at a small outdoor café, enjoying lunch while traffic drifted by. It was one of those simple, ordinary afternoons: sun warm, glasses sweating on the table, us laughing and sharing stories under an awning. Then I noticed Gaylynn's eyes shift toward a young man nearby. His clothes were worn, his hair unkempt, a tattered backpack slung low on his shoulders. I hadn't even noticed him, but Gaylynn saw him. Before taking a bite, she gathered together her food, put it in a box, stood up, and walked over. The aroma of tomatoes and fresh bread lingered as she folded the box shut, then placed it gently in his hands with a smile. "Here, sweetheart," she said, "you look like you might be hungry."

The young man's face lit with relief. He accepted the meal gratefully, shoulders softening as if someone had finally noticed he existed. I remember the way the traffic seemed to fade for a moment, the banter of engines replaced by the simple sound of gratitude in his quiet "thank you." When Gaylynn sat back down, I asked why she had given away her lunch so quickly. She looked at me with her trademark boldness and said, "Because I know how it feels to be hungry and not know where your next meal is coming from."

That was Gaylynn. Where others saw inconvenience or walked past, she saw need. Her heart recognized hunger, because she had known it herself.

There were countless other moments like that. A friend once gave her an old iPad, saying she had thought about buying a new one but knew Gaylynn would just give it away. She was right. Before long, Gaylynn had passed it on to someone who needed it more. To her, giving wasn't about loss; it was about trust. "Everything I've given away," she would say, "I've gotten back tenfold. God is good and always provides more than enough for me."

That belief—that generosity was never wasted—sustained her. It shaped her into a woman who lived in abundance even when she had little. Because Gaylynn had learned a valuable lesson through a life of hardships: Abundance isn't measured in bank accounts. It's measured in open hands and open hearts.

As her life in Florida settled into a steadier cadence, Gaylynn turned her attention toward the fractures that weighed most heavily: her family. Years of brokenness could not be undone quickly, but she longed for peace. Step by step, conversation by conversation, she began to rebuild. Some relationships responded to her efforts—small reconciliations marked by forgiveness and grace. Others stayed distant, wounds still too deep and raw. But the desire to mend what had been broken remained a powerful motivation.

Her journal pages bore witness to that struggle. She wrote of grace, of forgiveness, of the sting of rejection, of the belief for restoration. She wrestled with questions of how to love family who still carried sharp edges, and how to release anger when it rose. Over time, she learned that mending was not about forcing reconciliation but about opening herself to it. Each small victory, each phone call, each softening became another step forward.

Spiritually, she continued searching. Gaylynn had spent years exploring different paths to "enlightenment;" at one point even tattooing Mala beads on her wrist as a symbol of her quest. In her search, Buddhism had offered a measure of peace, but it never satisfied the longing at her core. In time, she came back to what she had always known deep down: Only God's love could provide the lasting acceptance for who she is that eluded her for so long. "God is love" (1 John 4:8). That truth took root in her again, stronger than before.

Watching her wander and return reminded me how often we all go searching for answers in places that quiet the noise for a while but never fill the emptiness. Only God's love can do that, and I saw that truth unfolding in her.

What she worked out privately on paper and in prayer began to spill over into her relationships and daily choices.

Her daughter's death continued to mark her life with a profound reminder: Say "I love you" every time you can. For Gaylynn, these parting words became sacred. She would end every phone call, every visit with an embrace or a phrase of love, knowing too well that tomorrow is never promised.

She also reached out intentionally to family members she had once held at a distance. She started speaking often with her half sister and half brother. She built a better relationship with her birth father, and she called her mother nearly every day. The conversations weren't always easy, but they mattered. I respected and even encouraged her willingness to keep trying, even with those who had wounded her most. Where I might have held on to bitterness, she chose to release it, again and again. Even as some relationships softened, others remained painfully distant. The fracture with her younger sister still weighed heavily, and though years had passed, the hollow never truly left. They had once been inseparable—leaning on each other through the worst of their childhood trials. Now, wordlessness had replaced those unspoken promises. Even with all the progress she made elsewhere, that unrepaired bond was proof that reconnecting and forgiveness rarely moves in a straight line. It was an absence that cut deeper than anger ever could—a reminder that some of the deepest wounds aren't loud, they're simply absent. Some doors open quickly; others stay closed on this side of heaven no matter how much you long to walk through them.

Gaylynn continues to focus on her own growth, using the lessons she's learned from her past to shape healthier relationships. Everything she has experienced—every heartbreak, every sorrow, and every moment of grace—continues to shape her approach to life, allowing her to build a better future for herself and others.

As her faith deepened, so did her pursuit of creating wholeness in body and spirit. Her relentless curiosity turned toward nutrition, health, and the connection between food and recovery. She began researching, studying, learning all she could about how lifestyle choices impact not only survival but thriving after cancer. What she discovered ignited a new passion: teaching others that recovery wasn't just medical; it was holistic.

She shared her findings freely. "Everything we need to know about living a healthy life is right there in the Bible," she would say. "God told us our bodies are a temple; we just need to take care of them according to what He says." For Gaylynn, nutrition became a ministry, a way to serve others walking their own roads through illness or loss. She taught that food could be medicine, that small changes could transform lives, that caring for the body was also a way of honoring the God who made it. Bowls of fruit in bright colors—mango, papaya, berries—nuts and seeds, natural herbs and spices became reminders that God had placed everything we need for restoring our bodies in creation itself. Her kitchen often smelled of lemons and ginger, sharp and bright, scents that reminded her of both the island she had left behind and the new life she was building.

On her long and winding road, Gaylynn had endured more than most—childhood trauma, loss, addiction, betrayal, disease. But through prayer, journaling, generosity, reconciliation, and her relentless search for God, she had found renewal. Florida became the canvas where she painted that new chapter: not free from challenges, but no longer held captive by them.

Gaylynn continues to live that way even now—her spirit radiant, glowing even, and her faith in God still growing, especially when tested, her heart remains open to what He has for her. She embodies the truth that the road to restoration is rarely simple, but always possible. And in her story is a lesson for all of us: that when we look back honestly, we can move forward with courage. That even after years of pain, God's love is strong enough to rebuild, restore, and renew.

Healing looked different now. It looked like resilience, sunshine, and the ocean at her feet.

CHAPTER 25

A MISSION EMERGING

"The two most important days in your life are the day you are born and the day you find out why." — *Mark Twain*

Gaylynn didn't stumble into the wellness world; it grew out of her own determination to heal. What began as a personal journey, rooted in years of trial, error, and relentless research, became something much larger than herself. Through every painful setback and every small breakthrough, she discovered a passion not only for her own restoration but for helping others find theirs.

She knows the toll of illness firsthand—the feeling of being trapped in a body that refuses to cooperate, the fear that every day might bring a new complication. That empathy runs deep in her, shaping the way she meets people where they are. Her calling isn't abstract; it comes from lived experience. She wants others to know they are not alone in their battles, just as she once felt utterly alone in hers.

Since Gaylynn's cancer battle, she now understands that health has never been about temporary fixes or quick diets. For her, it's about long-term change, sustainable habits, and the conviction that food can be medicine—truths learned firsthand. In every session she leads, whether with one person or in a group, she speaks of wellness as a way of life, rooted in God's design to nourish the body, steady the mind, and sharpen the spirit. Faith is never an afterthought. She teaches that prayer, nutrition, and movement belong together, woven into the same fabric. Living healthfully, she reminds her students, is less about appearances and more about honoring the God who created us.

"God didn't walk me through this life for me to be a mediocre person," she often says, her way of making sense of a life that rarely added up. It's become one of her guiding mantras. Those words hold meaning because they come from someone who has lived the trenches of loss, addiction, betrayal, and disease—and still found her way forward. She isn't content to merely endure; she is determined to thrive and bring others along with her.

In a small room, folding chairs lined up in uneven rows, Gaylynn stood in front of a group of mostly women who had signed up for one of her first in-person wellness class. Her "presentation" was nothing more than a few notes scribbled in her journal and a basket of groceries she had picked up that morning. She held up some dark leafy vegetables, explaining how foods God created in their natural state can fortify the body. She laughed as she demonstrated a quick stretch, her students laughing with her, the tension in the room dissolving. She often marveled at how teaching seemed to shape her as much as it did her students. Standing in front of others, she no longer felt reduced to illness but lifted by purpose. The low drone of the room, the shuffle of chairs, an occasional cough, and muted exchanges breaking the stillness as the class settled in became affirmations that her pain had not been wasted. Each person who showed up reminded her of the nights she had prayed for a reason to keep going, and here it was, unfolding before her eyes. By the end of that hour, people weren't just taking notes; they were leaning in, asking questions, confessing their own struggles.

I couldn't help but notice the contrast. Only a few years earlier, she had been the patient bowed under tubes and chemo, her body skeletal, her voice faint. Now here she stood—still marked by what she had endured, still carrying the imprint of suffering, but speaking with an authority born of those very trials. It was as if the sickness that once silenced her had been repurposed into a platform, her pain transformed into testimony.

Later, as sessions moved online, the scene looked different but carried the same energy. Her old iPhone, propped on a wobbly stack of books, became her pulpit. She joked about her "studio," which sometimes sent the phone sliding mid-call and gave students a sudden view of the ceiling—but no one minded. They weren't coming for polish; they were coming for Gaylynn's heart. Then, true to God's nature, provision came in ways she hadn't expected: a brand-new phone and iPad. Smiling, she told me, "I gave away my old iPad, and look, God returned it tenfold! Now I have a new phone *and* a new iPad!" For Gaylynn, it wasn't about the devices themselves—it was about what they represented. They were reminders of God's ongoing care, tangible signs of her belief that when she remained faithful, He always provided. She greeted each person who joined her screen by name, waving as they signed in from kitchens and living rooms. Sometimes a dog barked in the background or a grandparent wandered into view, and Gaylynn never missed a beat, turning interruptions into moments of connection. What she lacked in polish, she more than made up for in warmth and humor.

The demand for her guidance has grown steadily as word spreads. People see in her not only knowledge but authenticity. She doesn't present herself as an expert with all the answers, and she is the first to say she isn't a doctor, has no formal medical degree. What she offers is born of hard-earned wisdom: years of fighting for her health, hours spent poring over research, and lessons learned from trial and error. When someone comes to her, especially those facing cancer, one of the first things she urges them to do is pray. "Cancer hates a positive mindset," she tells them. "When you connect with God, everything begins to shift—your body, your spirit, your outlook."

She also teaches practical tools. One of her firm beliefs is that sugar fuels disease, and she encourages her students to keep a food log. "Write down everything you eat," she tells them. "You can't change what you won't face." For many, that simple act of awareness becomes a turning point.

In one session, a woman arrived burdened by fear of relapse after treatment. Her hands shook as she spoke, and tears fell before she could finish her first sentence. Gaylynn didn't rush into advice; instead, she listened, prayed with her, and reminded her that the road to wholeness is often winding, and rarely simple. By the end of their time together, the woman left lighter than she had come, carrying not only a food plan but the reassurance that she wasn't walking her road alone.

A man battling obesity met with her; his goal was to shed some pounds and begin to feel better. From the start, Gaylynn focused less on numbers and more on dignity. She reminded him that his worth wasn't tied to a scale and that caring for his body was a way of honoring the God who had created it. He began by keeping a food log, then taking short walks, celebrating each small victory instead of shaming himself for setbacks. Months later, he sent her a message: He had lost weight, yes, but more importantly, he had belief for the first time in years. "You didn't just teach me about food," he wrote. "You taught me how to believe again." For Gaylynn, that was the true measure of success: not pounds lost, but a life reclaimed.

Gaylynn treasures those words more than any number on a scale. Each story affirms her conviction that her work isn't about physical appearance; it's about giving people back their sense of worth, their belief that life can still hold joy.

Still, Gaylynn is the first to admit that her own road has been difficult. The calling she lives out today was shaped in the shadows of depression and doubt. There were days when she felt pulled under by despair, when her body ached and her spirit sagged, when old traumas haunted her with the thought that she would never fully climb out. In those moments, the temptation to give up was real. On the hardest days, even getting out of bed felt impossible. The heaviness of depression pressed down, her chest tight as though it remembered every surgery, every loss. She would sit in silence, staring at the blank page of her journal, unsure if she had anything left to say. Yet it was in those moments—when her pen finally moved, when a prayer finally broke the stillness—that she felt God meet her most tenderly. She was learning that a healthy life was not a steady climb upward but a series of steps—some faltering, some strong, all of them moving her forward.

She developed small daily rituals—morning prayer, journaling, and meditation—that became her armor. These practices didn't erase the pain, but they gave her steadiness to keep moving through it.

Not long ago, an unexpected health complication threatened to undo her progress. The setback could have sent her spiraling, but instead of crumbling, she surrendered it. "Lord, I don't understand, but I trust You," she prayed. Supported by her community and sustained by her enduring faith, she emerged stronger. Looking back, she came to believe those setbacks were often setups for breakthroughs.

In my church one Sunday, Pastor Chad V. said something that stayed with me: "When you realize God's given you a mission, you will fight harder to stay free—because someone else's freedom might be connected to yours." Later, I shared those words with Gaylynn, and they struck her like an arrow. She had long believed her life wasn't just about her own recovery, but hearing it spoken like that gave her a new clarity. Every time she taught a class, every time she prayed with someone over the phone, every time she shared her story, she was stepping into that calling.

Her mission is not tidy or easy. It costs her energy, time, and always more than a few tears. But each person who tells her, "You helped me believe again" or "I feel stronger because of you" makes it all worthwhile. Gaylynn has learned that her story is more than a testimony; it is an invitation. By showing up as she is, pain and all, she offers others a glimpse of what's possible. Watching her live this calling stirred something in me as well. I had seen the little girl who once carried the weight of everyone else's mistakes, the young woman who fought through heartbreak and loss, the patient bowed under illness. To now see her stand with open hands, offering a chance to dream to others, was nothing short of remarkable. It reminded me that none of us are meant to walk through pain alone. Our stories are threads in a larger tapestry, meant to hold and comfort one another. Her courage pulls so many others forward, just as it now reaches for the reader who holds these pages. And for me, it is a reminder that telling her story is also part of my own calling—to bear witness, so that faith is multiplied.

The shadows of Gaylynn's past, once a burden shaping every decision, no longer dictate her life. Instead, she is actively building toward a future aligned with peace, faith, and service. She knows the path is not perfect; she still endures days of doubt, moments of weariness, endless questions for God. But she moves forward and thanks God every morning for another day to work for Him.

Her struggles became the blueprint for her mission. With every person she touches, she has proven that the process for getting better wasn't meant to be hoarded; it was always meant to be shared. Yet beneath that calling, sorrow and struggle still lived side by side—chemo and surgeries on one hand, and the ache of a daughter gone too soon on the other. Both demanded more of her spirit. Even so, she pressed on, carrying loss with her but refusing to let it silence the possibilities she now offered so freely.

She isn't just surviving anymore; she is leading others to rise.

STANDING FIRM IN FREEDOM

These closing pages offer a glimpse into the healing and restoration Gaylynn has come to embrace.

"I am here today because of prayer warriors lifting me up." — Gaylynn Kapri

Gaylynn has learned much about resilience, health, and mending, and now she shares what she's discovered with others. The pain, the suffering, the countless hours of wondering if she would ever make it through—they are no longer just hers. They belong to the multitude of souls she's met along the way, people carrying their own battles and looking for light. As she often says, "If I can help even one person find their way out of the shadows, then everything I've been through will have been worth it."

There was a time when Gaylynn couldn't see past the isolation and darkness that surrounded her. So often it felt like the crushing load of the world had pressed her beyond repair. But today she stands not only flourishing, but more resolved than anyone—including herself—ever thought possible. It wasn't easy. The road was long, and the wounds were profound. Yet through it all, she came to see that God wasn't finished with her. Again and again, He pulled her from the ashes, moving her forward on the path He had paved for her long before she could see it. As she says, "I have carried the scars of childhood trauma, the death of my daughter, and cancer for so long, but now, I carry my purpose. And it's a purpose that has set me free."

She no longer fears the challenges that lie ahead. Every obstacle is another chance to rise, to push further, to show others what is possible. Gaylynn will not be silenced by fear or chained by the past. She keeps moving forward—determined, relentless. She is not just an overcomer. She is a warrior.

Every setback has only underscored that her mission is bigger than herself. Her calling is not only about her own renewal, but about helping others believe they can break free from the heaviness of their past, find peace in the present, and step boldly into the future. She teaches that bodily mending is not a final destination but a lifelong walk—one that requires prayer, dedication, and perseverance. With God, transformation is possible for anyone.

Throughout her life, Gaylynn often reacted impulsively to challenges, roadblocks, and fears that seemed overwhelming. Though moments of panic still come, she has learned to pause, to breathe, and to turn first to God. She knows now that strength and wisdom come most clearly when she seeks Him before anything else.

Despite being diagnosed with stage 4 colon cancer—a disease doctors described as incurable—Gaylynn lived to hear the words "no evidence of disease" from her compassionate doctor. Against every prognosis, against every warning, she became cancer-free. Her surgeon, who had once prepared her for the worst, could only marvel. Everyone around her, including her medical team, call it nothing less than miraculous. She points to prayer, lifestyle changes, and sheer persistence—but always, she says, it was God's hand that carried her through. Her recovery is a living testimony that miracles still happen.

She knows she is where she is today because so many prayed for her. Now she is the one praying for others, every day. She found her own Batphone.

"I look back at the woman who once thought she'd never survive," she says. "I look at the scars, the losses, the failures, and I see them for what they are: not signs of weakness, but badges of honor.

Now, I want to walk this path with others—through prayer, healing, and helping them find their purpose."

If there's one thing Gaylynn desires readers carry from her story, it's this: No matter how broken you feel, with God you have the power to rebuild. Wholeness is not a finish line but a daily walk, one step at a time.

Today Gaylynn reaches countless people through her testimony and her passion for wellness. She continues working with individuals and groups, guiding them toward healthier choices and a deeper walk with God. She is living proof that when you tend both body and spirit, you can become unstoppable. As one student shared, "Gaylynn has saved my life. I had diabetes and was obese. Through meeting with her regularly, I developed a deeper relationship with God, lost weight, and am now off all my medications. I credit her and the miraculous works God has done through her." Another wrote, "She didn't just teach me how to eat better—she taught me how to live better."

The road has been long, the wounds profound, the battles fierce. Yet through it all, Gaylynn has learned that freedom is not the absence of pain but the presence of God in every step forward. In that truth, she walks today—whole, restored, and free, because somebody prayed. And as I write these words, I know I am one of those voices—one of the many who kept the line open, believing God was not done with her yet.

The trials of this life didn't break her. They revealed God's light in her.

EPILOGUE

LIVING A BEAUTIFUL LIFE

"The best and most beautiful things in the world cannot be seen or even touched—they must be felt with the heart."
— Helen Keller

Telling someone else's story is an honor and sacred undertaking. It requires reverence, honesty, and a willingness to sit with memories that don't always offer clean resolutions. There were moments in writing this book when I had to step away from the keyboard, close my eyes, and breathe deeply—because the burden of what I was holding was heavy, and it wasn't even mine to carry.

Looking back on everything Gaylynn has endured—and everything she's become—I see the fingerprints of God's grace woven through every chapter. Grace in the moments she should have been crushed but wasn't. Grace in the people who showed up when she needed them most. Grace in the fact that she's still here to tell her story. It reminds me that survival is only the beginning; what comes after is where the real transformation happens.

I didn't write this book to make sense of her pain. Pain rarely fits into tidy explanations. I wrote it because her life testifies to something greater: the presence of God in the ordinary, in the broken, in the waiting. I have watched her rise from more losses than I can count—childhood trauma, devastating family turmoil, the unimaginable grief of losing a daughter, and then the fight for her own life. And still, she rises.

As her cousin, I've walked many of those roads beside her. I've stood on the outside looking in, helpless at times, constant in prayer, and yet always aware of something unshakable in her spirit. Writing this story has reminded me of the kind of resolve that lives in women like Gaylynn: the bold power that meets hardship head-on and refuses to be silenced. It's a resolve born of relentless faith and a God who refuses to let go. But faith doesn't promise smooth roads, only the assurance that we are never walking alone.

Reflecting on Gaylynn's incredible journey and the impact she's had on so many lives, I'm reminded of a recent lunch we shared with my two granddaughters, who, like Gaylynn and me, are cousins just four years apart. We laughed and swapped stories—funny moments, crazy experiences, and everything in between. Then my oldest grand-daughter looked at me and asked, "Nana, do you think we'll be like you and Gaylynn when we grow up?" Her question pulled me back through decades of shared memories and made me realize that even as we live through our own battles and triumphs, the love and connection we share can echo through future generations.

As you've read her story, I pray you've approached it with an open heart and compassion. We all have chapters in our lives that are hard for others to understand. Gaylynn's choices, though not always easy to comprehend, were made with the knowledge and strength she had in those moments. As Priscilla Shirer writes in *Fervent*, "There's not one of us—not one—who can't stare back into our past and wish a hundred times we'd done a hundred things differently."[1] And yet, those choices become part of our testimony. They shape the way we see the world, and they shape the way God meets us in our need. Let us also remember the words of Jesus in John 8:7: "Let any one of you who is without sin be the first to throw a stone at her." It is not ours to throw stones, but to extend the same grace we ourselves have received.

---

1   Priscilla Shirer, *Fervent: A Woman's Battle Plan to Serious, Specific, and Strategic Prayer* (B&H Books, 2015), 100.

Today, Gaylynn continues to pour into others. Her scars are not hidden; they have become road maps for those she now walks alongside. She listens without judgment. She offers a seat at the table to anyone who needs it. She gives people permission to be both broken and beautiful at the same time.

This memoir does not end with perfection; it ends with presence. With the truth that God never left her, not in the darkest valleys nor on the brightest mountaintops. It ends with the knowing that survival wasn't the goal. Transformation was.

> *I have made peace with all the versions of myself—every scar, every heartache, the fighter and the lover; because each of these parts has shaped me into the woman I am today. All glory and honor goes to God!*
> *— Gaylynn Kapri*

And to you, dear reader, whether you carry wounds, doubts, or the strain of your own valleys, may this story remind you: God is not done with you. Not even close. And now that you've seen Gaylynn's journey, may you hear those words for yourself: Get up. He's not done with you. Live your beautiful life.

She fought. I wrote. And together, we remembered.

ACKNOWLEDGMENTS

This book would not exist without the extraordinary strength, perseverance, and tenacity of Gaylynn Kapri. Her story is one of survival, yes—but even more, one of redemption. I am deeply honored that she entrusted me with the sacred task of helping to share her life's journey.

Gaylynn's willingness to speak truth, revisit painful chapters, and offer hope to others is nothing short of courageous. Through every hardship and healing moment, her faith in God remained the thread holding it all together, even when she didn't see it for herself.

I also give heartfelt thanks to those who supported this project through prayer, encouragement, and love: To my husband, for giving me the space to write, even when it meant dinner was late, cold, or sometimes forgotten altogether.

To my family: especially my girls, BreeAnn and Staci—for always being my first readers and sounding boards. You helped illuminate my path, especially when doubt lingered.

Above all, I thank my heavenly Father, who authors every story with purpose, even the ones written through pain. May this book be a testament to His faithfulness and a beacon of hope for those still walking through their own valleys.

And to you, dear reader, may you be reminded that beauty can rise from ashes, and healing is never too far from reach.

To Gaylynn—Thank you for allowing your life to become a vessel of hope and healing. Your light shines through every page, and I can only hope I've honored your story with the voice and justice it deserves. In the rush, the rewrites, or those moments when your logic left me scrambling to catch up, I hope I made you proud.

This is squirrel leader to chipmunk . . . we did it!

> *"The light shines in the darkness, and the*
> *darkness has not overcome it." — John 1:5*

ABOUT THE AUTHORS

LaVonne M. Chastain is the author of this memoir and the cousin of Gaylynn Kapri, whose life story is at the heart of this book. Drawing from decades of shared memories, intimate conversations, and deep personal connection, LaVonne brings Gaylynn's journey to life with honesty, reverence, and love.

LaVonne lives in California with her husband and two dogs. Their children and grandchildren live close by, and time with family remains one of her greatest joys. She lives by a simple but unwavering mantra she learned from her adopted father: faith and family first.

Gaylynn Kapri is the central voice and soul of this story. Her life has been shaped by trauma, triumph, tragedy, and transformation. A mother, survivor, and woman of faith, her journey continues to inspire hope in others.

After enduring unimaginable loss and illness, Gaylynn has made it her mission to walk alongside those facing their own valleys. She shares her story not for sympathy, but to shine a light for those still finding their way through shadows.

She currently resides in Florida and continues to travel, speak, and minister through her testimony, living each day with courage, authenticity, and tenacity.

Together, their bond and trust form the foundation of this deeply personal and powerful memoir.

www.ingramcontent.com/pod-product-compliance
Lightning Source LLC
Chambersburg PA
CBHW021038130626
46552CB00005B/1912